POTTERY

A Basic Manual

POTTERY

A Basic Manual

CORA PUCCI

Photographs by Peter Hunsberger

Little, Brown and Company — Boston–Toronto

T 06/74

First Edition

The drawings in this book are by the author.

All photographs in this book were taken by Peter Hunsberger with the exception of that on page 59, which was taken by David Lang.

Photographs taken at the Old Schwamb Mill, Arlington, Massachusetts.

The chart of Temperature Equivalents for Orton Standard Pyrometric Cones (page 149) is reproduced with the permission of the Edward Orton Jr. Ceramic Foundation, 1445 Summit Street, Columbus, Ohio 43201.

Library of Congress Cataloging in Publication Data

Pucci, Cora.
    Pottery: a basic manual.

    (Little, Brown crafts series)
    Bibliography: p.
    1. Pottery craft. I. Title.
TT920.P8   738.1   74-1068
ISBN 0-316-72110-7
ISBN 0-316-72111-5 (pbk.)

Published simultaneously in Canada by Little, Brown & Company (Canada) Limited
Printed in the United States of America

To two people who played an important part in my development:

My brother,
who early in my life opened my consciousness
to the whole world of art, and

Anne Magbie,
my first pottery teacher and close friend,
who was always supportive of me
in my early efforts
to shape a life both independent and productive.

The Little, Brown Crafts Series is designed and published for the express purpose of giving the beginner—usually a person trained to use his head, not his hands—an idea of the basic techniques involved in a craft, as well as an understanding of the inner essence of that medium. Authors were sought who do not necessarily have a "name" but who thoroughly enjoy sharing their craft, and all their sensitivities to its unique nature, with the beginner. Their knowledge of their craft is vital, although it was realized from the start that one person can never teach all the techniques available.

The series helps the beginner gain a sense of the spirit of the craft he chooses to explore, and gives him enough basic instruction to get him started. Emphasis is laid on creativity, as crafts today are freed from having to be functional; on process, rather than product, for in the making is the finding; and on human help, as well as technical help, as so many prior teaching tools have said only "how" and not "why." Finally, the authors have closed their books with as much information on "next steps" as they could lay their hands on, so that the beginner can continue to learn about the craft he or she has begun.

Gerald Clow

Acknowledgments

I heartily thank Peter Hunsberger for his superb photography. His sensitive grasp of pottery-making comes through in the working photographs, many of which were taken from difficult positions over my head, over my shoulder, under my arm, to get the clearest possible views. My thanks also to Carole Thaxton, who not only typed the manuscript but involved herself in the project in a very giving and delightful way; Franz Browne for lending us his typewriter and opening his air-conditioned home at the height of a persistent heat wave so we could complete the last stages of the manuscript in comfort; Cy Lipsitt and Tele Bjork, who took the time to supply me with some text as well as photographs of their studios and work; Nadine Hurst, Marlis Schratter, Tom Joanides, Kathleen Ingoldsby for providing me with photographs of their studios and work; the friends at the Old Schwamb Mill in Arlington, Massachusetts, where I have my studio, for their support and co-operation; my personal friends, who made themselves available to me whenever I needed either help or advice; and above all, the editor, Richard McDonough, and his assistant, Leslie Arnold, for their many hours of patient help.

Introduction

I was very lucky when I was first learning to make pottery. My friend Anne Magbie, who later became my teacher, allowed me to use her basement studio when she was not working in it herself. It was there, when I was quietly alone with the clay, that I began to experience and become aware of what I now call a relationship with clay. I didn't realize at first that I was being drawn just, by the feel of clay in my hands, and the occasional but rewarding moments when I accidentally hit upon a sense of being integrated with clay and potter's wheel. Certainly, I was making things, or trying to, but soon I became interested in the process of making. And so it was that between experiencing my medium, the clay, so closely, and feeling that I was an intimate part of the process of pottery-making, the question of commitment ceased to exist.

When I worked in that studio, I never kept what I made. Somehow I felt free of the mania to keep everything. The studio was my practice house. Whenever I concluded an afternoon of practicing, I always had the very contented feeling that I had had a long, meaningful conversation. I found without practicing—without allowing myself to go through the mistakes I was going to make anyway over and over again until I found solutions—that no matter how much I loved pottery or how much talent I thought I had, I would get nowhere. I deeply respect practicing—over and over and over again. In the seemingly repetitive act of drawing up cylinder after cylinder, I found myself slowly relaxing my limbs and body, but at the same time discovering a tough and powerful core somewhere in the middle of me that was the force pulling the pots. It is difficult to explain this feeling, but I will throughout this book attempt to do so in different words, because I believe strongly that you cannot experience pottery-making well without an awareness of and a striving toward this state. I also believe, and have so observed in students with whom I have worked, that practice is the vehicle that brings you from one stage to another of the total experience of making, and that the potter never gives up practice. It is for the beginner and the experienced as well.

Contents

PART ONE

SUGGESTED BOOKS AND PUBLICATIONS

part

1

Clay

Throw: to make a pot on the potter's wheel.

It is with clay that the potter makes forms. But just being able to make something, to build a pot, to throw a pot on the wheel, to produce nice pottery—though it takes long practice to develop the skills to do these things—is not the only important goal. This is by no means a complete book on pottery or on learning pottery. It is my intention to expose you to some of the basic, age-old, well-loved practices in pottery-making with which I am familiar and to provide you with some kind of plan for learning and practicing these techniques until they become second nature.

But I have another wish, and that is to be able to transmit to you the importance of a special feeling for the clay you work with. I don't mean that it should be this clay or that clay, but that when you are working with clay, you become very conscious of something in your hands, and that something is affecting you and you are affecting it. At all times you must be aware of this wet

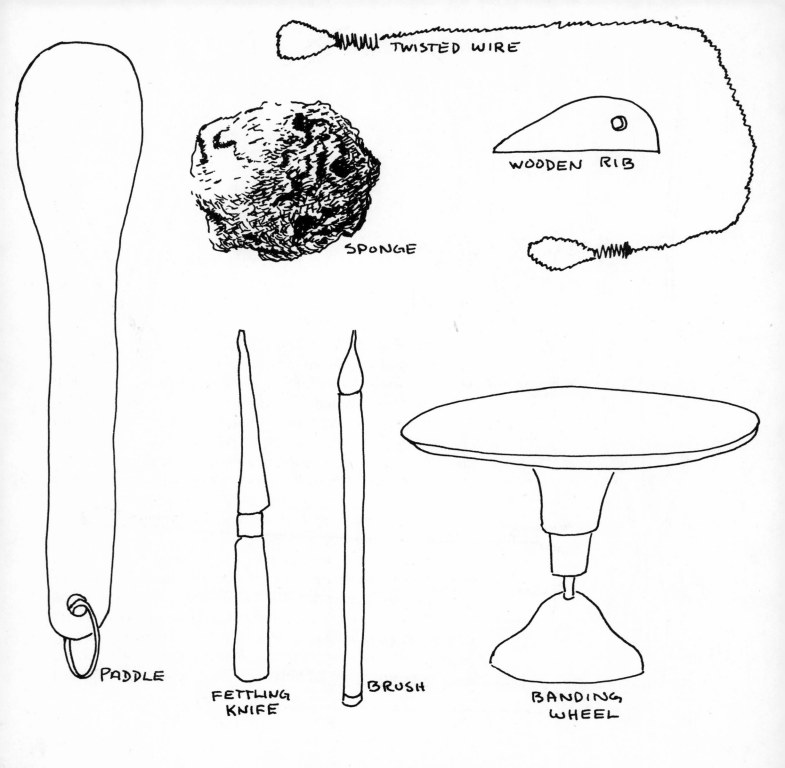

TWISTED WIRE

SPONGE

WOODEN RIB

PADDLE

FETTLING
KNIFE

BRUSH

BANDING
WHEEL

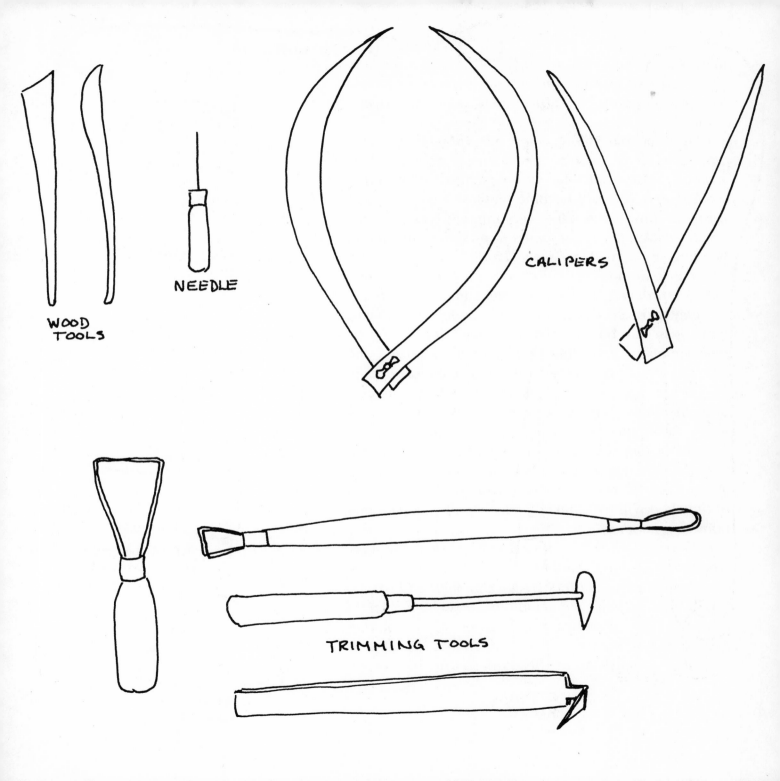

WOOD
TOOLS

NEEDLE

CALIPERS

TRIMMING TOOLS

mass with which you are going to develop a relationship. You will find it is alive, that it seems to have a
temperament of its own. There are certain laws govern-
ing it.

Clay is pliable, plastic, movable, vulnerable, tough,
wet, dry, slimy, spongy, heavy, gray, brown, white,
crumbly, sticky, but it has its limits, and as you start to
work with it you will become more aware of and surprised at these limits. It is very important to know the
nature of clay if you are going to establish any kind of
working rapport with and respect for it.

Because of the nature of clay, the act of making pottery goes in cycles. Before a potter can make anything,
the clay must be prepared. Some people like to mix
their own clay body, some will have it dry-mixed by
their suppliers, and others will have it wet-mixed and
ready to use. I suggest that you find a ceramics supplier
in your vicinity and start working with a stoneware clay
body they have at hand. Buy about a hundred pounds.
If you know any potters in your area, ask them for a
handful of their clay body and compare the feel of it
with the clay you have just bought. Feel as many clays
as you have access to, and after working a short period
of time you will find that you have a preference for one
body over another.

Different clays have different maturing temperatures
when they are fired. Earthenware is a low-fire red body
maturing at about 2000 degrees Fahrenheit and can be
used for large, unglazed sculptures or with very bright
low-fire glazes. Stoneware is a high-fire body maturing
at about 2200 to 2500 degrees Fahrenheit. Because of
its high durability and the beautiful soft richness of the

Clay body: a formula of different clays mixed
to produce a desirable working clay.

Maturing temperature: for clay, the temperature at which the body reaches its highest state
of hardness.

6

glazes used at such high temperatures, it is most often used for functional ware, as well as large sculptural pieces.

Porcelain fires at even higher temperatures than stoneware. It is a white clay of very fine quality. The finest ware made of porcelain is actually translucent. Modern potters have for a long time been using porcelain to make sculptures, funky ware, and of course, fine tableware.

Potters often like to design their own clay bodies, that is, they create a mixture of three or four clay bodies that together give a desired body consistency: open and coarse, closed and fine, or something in between.

Wedging Board

Clay that comes directly out of the box—the wet mix—is not completely ready to work with. It has to be wedged.

If you have ever been in a pottery studio, or if you have taken a course somewhere, you will then be aware of the need for a wedging surface. Maybe you already have a wedging board, but if you don't, you can easily make one. The point of the wedging board is to have a surface to which the clay will not stick as you are kneading it. This surface can be wood, plaster, the underside of an oilcloth, any stiff cloth, such as canvas, stretched and nailed to a sturdy table top, even a slab of slate or marble, if you happen to have these stones around. The size wedging board you have will of course depend on where you will be working. Wherever you work, be sure your board is secure and steady so you

Wedging: kneading clay to mix and push out air bubbles.

can wedge and knead freely. Here is one idea for making a board:

Take an old drawer from a chest of drawers or an old kitchen table and nail a 2" x 4" x 24" board into one corner. Screw a hook into the top part of the board and one onto the drawer and tightly secure a thin wire between them. If you do not have access to a drawer, make a box with 1" x 4" x 24" boards for the sides and a base of any piece of scrap wood or quarter-inch plywood.

Buy a hundred-pound sack of molding plaster from any lumber or construction supply house. Before mixing the plaster, be certain that the seams in the box are tight. If they are not, cover every seam by pushing a coil of clay into it. Now you are ready to mix the plaster. Take a large plastic basin, fill it half full of cool water (hot water will cause the plaster to set too fast), and start to sieve large handfuls of plaster into it through your fingers. Keep doing this until the plaster no longer sinks to the bottom and a thin smattering of it sits on the top. Place your hand in and under the mixture and agitate, mixing plaster and water thoroughly and breaking any remaining lumps with your fingers. Then pour the mixture into the box until it becomes even with the edge. If you need more plaster, simply repeat the process. There is no need to wash out the basin each time you mix. When you are finished, let the leftover plaster set in the bottom of the basin for about half an hour. When it is set, tap it out and you have a plaster *bat* or base on which to start building your first pots.

Any plaster stuck to the sides of the basin will easily

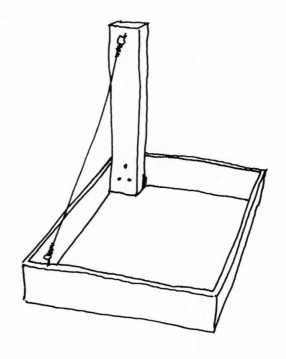

Bat: a base of wood or plaster on which to work.

pop off by tapping. Make some more plaster bats. You will see that you can vary the size bat by the basin you use. Square bats can be poured into a cardboard box lined with aluminum foil or Saran Wrap. Bats should be under two inches thick.

Because clay is made of minute particles or crystals very much in the shape of shingles on a roof (each shingle being about 1/50,000th of an inch), water is needed to hold the particles together. Wedging helps work the water into the clay. If you watch somebody wedging clay, you will notice there is a rhythm and a consistency in the process. This is the action that helps align the particles, which at first were helter-skelter. The particles become more and more lubricated and aligned with one another and the plastic quality of the clay is enhanced.

Wedging

Wedging pushes the air bubbles out of the mass and mixes the clay to a more even consistency.

Take a large lump of clay, filling both your hands, and start pushing into the lump from above. Keep moving the clay onto its various sides and pushing down (but

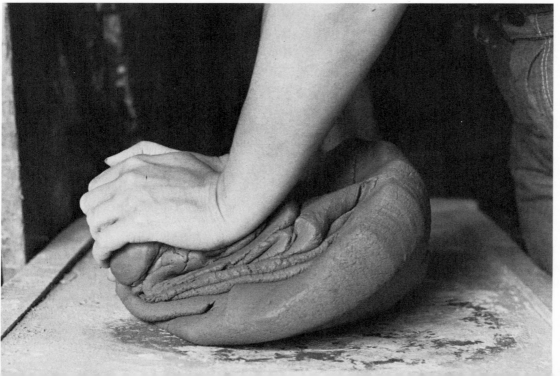

not flattening the lump) at each turn. This action pushes the air bubbles out. The photographs show a spiral motion. Start to wedge in slow motion, lifting the lump, turning it, and pushing down with both heels of your hands. When you do this in a rhythm, the lump shows a spiral design. Always keep in mind that you must never flatten the lump into a pancake. Work up a rhythm, or rocking motion, as you lift and push down.

Wedging by Cutting

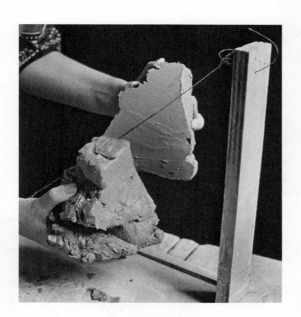

Very often the clay you have available to you is of uneven consistency. Some parts are hard and some are soft. Wedging by cutting and mixing is the best way to bring the body to an even consistency.

Take a medium-size lump and cut it in half on the wire of your wedging board. Slap one part down hard on the board and the other half hard onto the first one. Any air bubbles near the surface of the ends will burst. Do this about one dozen times. The cutting action helps mix the clay thoroughly.

The Limits of Clay

Try some of these simple experiments:

Take a lump of clay no larger than a golf ball. Squeeze it, knead it, roll it around in your hands, roll it around on the table, break it up into pieces, and pack them together again, continuing to do these things for about ten minutes. At the end of ten minutes, look at your lump.

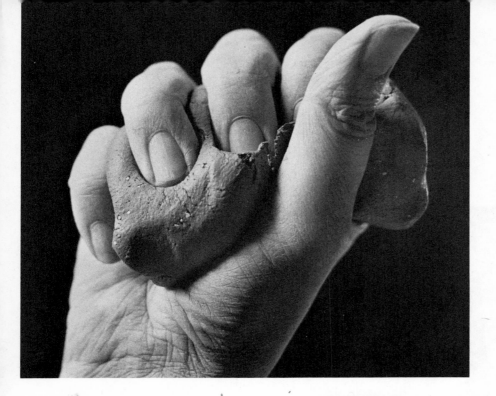

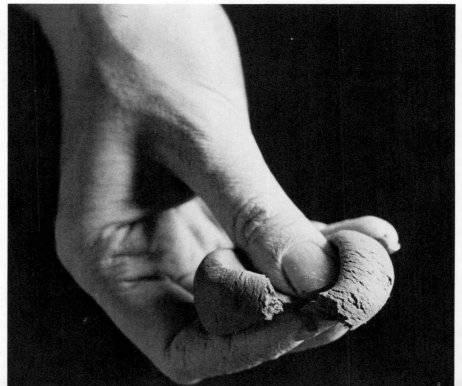

Does it look as wet as when you first started? No. The moisture in the clay has already begun to leave it and the clay is starting to crack. If you continue to manipulate the lump for another half hour, you will end up with crumbs.

You can see that clay particles are held together by water.

Take another lump the same size as the former and squeeze it hard between your thumb and first two fingers. If you squeeze hard enough, your fingers will reach each other and the edges of the clay will show openings in it. By squeezing the center of the lump, you have pushed the particles to another position — outward. As these particles move outward, they push other particles and so on until the particles on the outer rim separate.

When clay is squeezed too hard, a weakness will be created by the extreme separation in the particles and the clay splits.

Take a two- or three-pound lump and flatten it out on the table with your hand. Then take a rolling pin and start to roll it out, bearing down hard on the rolling pin until the slab of clay sticks to the table and the rolling pin. Try to get a feel for when the clay showed you that it was being pushed and stretched mercilessly.

When a slab of clay is rolled out with too much uneven pressure, the moisture will be squeezed out onto the table and rolling pin, trapping the clay onto them, causing it to stick and tear. When a slab of clay needs to be thinned with a rolling pin or broomstick, the action of the stick should be at an angle down and forward. Also, the clay should frequently be lifted from the table to give it freedom of movement as it is being rolled out.

Take a one-pound lump of clay and squeeze it out into a rope. Then continue to roll it out on the table, at the same time observing what is happening to it. Is it flat all of a sudden? Does it have thick and thin parts? Did it break? Now roll out another coil, this time concentrating carefully on what your hands are actually doing to cause the clay to flatten, weaken, and break. Try to figure out a way to correct this.

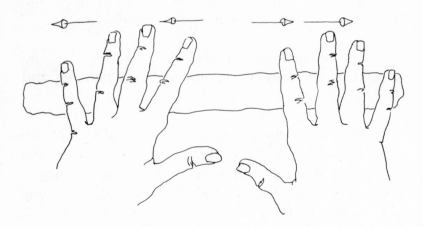

When making a coil, you want to move the particles outward without separating them entirely. As you roll the clay on the table, pull both hands outward, gently drawing the clay with you. Do not press too hard.

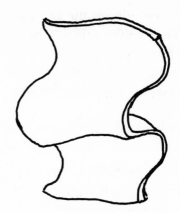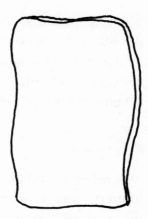

Roll out a slab of clay about 12″ x 12″ x ½″. Try to stand it on its edge. What happens? If it slumps down, cut the slab to about 10″ x 10″ and try to stand it again. Keep cutting it until the slab stands without slumping. Roll out another 12″ x 12″ slab and let it air-dry for about two hours. Then try to stand it on its edge. How dry is the clay? Should you have waited longer for it to dry?

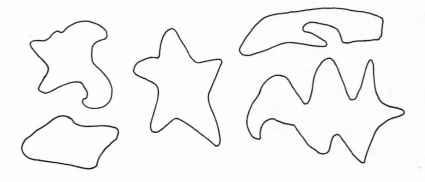

Take a small lump of clay and gently squeeze it out to

a flat shape—any kind of silhouette, letting the edge of the clay determine the shape. What do your fingers have to do to reach the shape? Are the edges cracking? Try to figure out what to do to avoid the cracking. Do several of these silhouettes and let them dry. Save them.

Play with Clay

Sometimes ideas are born by just taking any size lump of clay—a size that will fit into your hands—rolling it around in your hands, on the table, squeezing it, shaping the lump in any way that you imagine, each time observing what kind of form emerges, what kind of feeling this form evokes in you, what it seems to be saying.
Try this:

Take a lump of clay that feels comfortable in your hands. Start by very gently squeezing it as though you want to pull forms out of it. Then close your eyes, still playing with the lump, doing to it whatever comes into your head. Put that lump aside and do the same with another lump. Do this with about five lumps, each time working faster and faster. Now, look at your forms, even draw them—or only the parts of them that may please you. Observe them for their moods, their gestures. What are their moods? Somber, happy, funny, menacing, overbearing, light, heavy? This is their atmosphere. What are their gestures? Are they dancing, bowing, laughing, leaping, sprawling, balleting, squatting? This is their feeling, the motion you have given them.

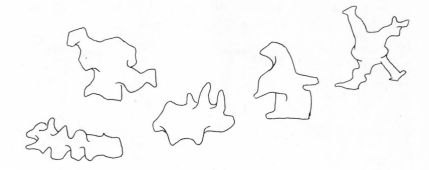

This is the kind of exercise you can do over and over again, and as you get deeper into pottery-making, you will find it an ever more meaningful activity. It shows you what forms are appealing to you, what stays with you. It reveals to you where you are at the time you are doing it. The shapes change either radically or ever so slightly as you change and grow.

Playing with the clay in this manner is something I have never stopped doing. It shows me what forms and gestures I'm responding to and it opens the way to finding an expression that may be new to me. Often I will fire one of the forms that especially speaks to me and keep it lying around my studio for weeks and months before I go back to it and maybe develop the idea further.

This little sculpture seemed to form itself one day as I was working on a large handbuilt pot. There were pieces of clay on the table near my work, and I started spontaneously to play with them. Two little bits of clay looked to me as though they were made for each other. I played with them, sticking them together and pulling little forms out of them. I glazed and fired the piece and let it sit on a shelf for many months before I went

back to it. Finally, after trying to build it in different proportions and sizes, I simply blew it up almost a hundred times its original size, ending up with a three-foot sculpture.

Keep on Playing

Inspiration can come from anywhere. When you embark on a life of pottery-making, you enter the world of form. Suddenly you realize that everything you touch, let alone see, has a form. Most of these things are not even pots. Some are beautiful, and some are ugly. They interact with other objects, with you, with the space they are in. They displace space. We are surrounded by many forms that please the eye—some of the architecture around us, sculptures, pottery and china, even industrial forms, machines and machine parts and, of course, forms in nature.

Open your eyes to all the forms surrounding you.

Look up from this page, sit back, take a deep breath, and very slowly start to look at what is around you. At first, observe each thing by itself. Forget what its function is and concentrate on its form, texture, color. Think that you are touching it, running your finger all around it, drawing it. Go to the next thing and do the same. Now go back and start to look at large groups of things, like a group of plants on the mantel and near the fireplace or a cluster of furniture. Take in the view without hurrying, concentrating on the group as a whole. Notice the spaces between things, imagining that these spaces are solid, too. Start to get a feeling about the spaces—are they too confined, too broad, too repetitive, monotonous, agitated? You may even want to change the positions of things until the interaction between them suits you.

This is a game you can play anywhere, even in the subway, a waiting room, the supermarket. You may ask, "Does this have anything to do with pottery?" It does. Though this kind of mental playing may not help you actually make a pot — only technique and practice will help you do that — it will help you become aware of the form of an object, not only its use. It will make you aware that as an object displaces space and relates to another object in space it creates a psychological effect on you; that some objects are pleasing to you, some are not, and you will begin to wonder why this is so. If you are going to work in a visual medium, then your visual perceptions must be sharpened, and as you continue to make pottery, you will become more acutely in tune with the world of form.

Nature, of course, is full of forms. Keep stones of different shapes around you all the time. Look at them, feel them, draw them. Pottery is very close to natural forms; it becomes hard, durable, sometimes smooth like a stone. The shapes of pottery are simple as a stone is simple. Pottery shapes are full and tight as stones are full and tight.

For three weeks in the summer of 1967, I attended a session at Haystack Mountain School for Crafts in Deer Island, Maine, where I was lucky enough to have Karen Karnes as a teacher. Not only was Karen a great inspiration to me both as a person and teacher, but so was the nature around me — the abundance of rocks, huge

and small, the trees, the sea. My visual perception became so heightened, I could actually sense life in rocks. Their forms became so alive for me that I was practically conversing with them. You may experience this with seashells, plants, flowers, or animals. These feelings you may have can infuse a certain kind of life into your work. These inspirations, then, can put form to some of your fantasies. Let these fantasies out.

Ask yourself these questions:

1. What attracts you when you are out on the street?
2. What are some of the things you loved when you were a child? Make a list of these things right now.
3. What were some of the spontaneous little gifts that your parents or other members of your family brought you when you were a little kid?
4. Did you ever play with the food on your plate, building scenes with it?
5. Did you ever play with your chewing gum and make things with it?
6. Did you ever feel if you talked to an animal long enough, it would talk back to you?
7. Did you ever take a lot of old clothes and rags and make a costume out of them?
8. Did you ever dress a stick to make a doll out of it?
9. Can you remember some of the daydreams of your childhood?
10. Can you imagine living without fantasies?

My first teacher always used to ask me what I was feeling whenever she saw me absentmindedly playing with a small piece of clay. Many times I could not answer her. But I knew somewhere inside me that it was an important question, and its importance became clearer to me with time. Her question stayed with me, teaching me to observe my movements when working with clay, to free my fantasies and to be aware of their strength in my work, to concentrate on what I am doing and to ask myself that same question more often. Fantasies are not to be avoided. As you work, you will find that apart from the general motivation of just wanting to learn to make pottery there is another motivation, borne by your fantasies and experiences, that connects you to your work and opens the flow from you to the clay. I cannot imagine living without fantasies.

Before going on, think about these questions.

1. What is it about pottery that attracts you to it?
2. Why do you want to get your hands into clay?
3. What is it you want to form with the clay?
4. What are your fantasies when you think about doing pottery?
5. What does pottery mean to you?

Can you draw the answers to these questions? Can you write them? If at this very moment you feel you cannot, don't worry. These questions will stay with you, and as you learn pottery and practice it, the answers will probably emerge quietly.

Handbuilding

There are three basic methods you need to know to do handbuilding (pottery without a wheel): the pinch, the coil, the slab. I want to take each method and discuss it with you, first showing the technique of each one and then providing you with working sessions that will give you a chance to develop a disciplined working relationship with your clay and open you to better possibilities of expression.

Pinch

Wedge up a lump of clay (about two and a half pounds). Take five smaller lumps from it, each weighing about a quarter of a pound or less, keeping them covered with a soft plastic sheet as you work on one lump at a time. Hold the smallest lump in the palm of one hand. Make a hole in it with the thumb of the other hand and come out at the other end. Start to squeeze the clay gently between your four fingers and thumb, turning the lump as you squeeze and keeping the shape of a tube. As you are squeezing, try to draw the clay up so that you are also lengthening the tube, always concentrating on the shape with which you are going to finish. Keep doing this until the wall is about a quarter-inch thick. When you have finished, observe the result. Is it a shape other than a tube? If so, try to figure out what you did. Did you squeeze one side to death? This action would overstretch it. Once a wall is overstretched you cannot unstretch it. Did one side come out lopsided? You must have pulled more on that side.

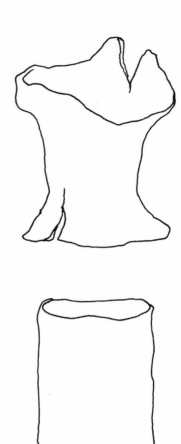

Now, go on to another lump. Make a hole through and through, and try to make another tube, perhaps wider than the first, or narrower. Before you start working, be still for a moment, imagine the shape you want, and keep focused on that shape. Start to work slowly, at all times concentrating on and feeling the shape you want. If you find the shape leaving you, close your eyes and bring it back into your mind, at the same time working slowly. When you are finished, observe what you have done. If you were able to concentrate and work slowly, thinking about your finger movements, you probably will have a simple tube shape. If not, do not worry.

Take a third lump. Make an opening through and through, and start pinching. This time, give the tube a shape. Try to make it as round as you can without enlarging the openings any more. Think about how you are going to put roundness into the lump and use your fingers to follow your ideas. You will find that in order to do this, your fingers will have to pull, push, and pack the clay together to get the shape you want. Squeezing

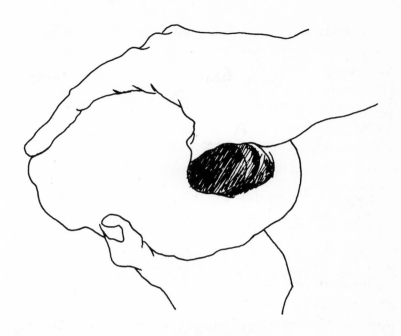

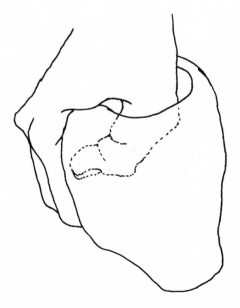

alone is not enough. If you want to push the shape out further, then your thumb on the inside must gently push or stretch the clay outward while your fingers on the outside meet the pressure and support the clay, preventing it from cracking and breaking. As you learn how much to push the clay out, you will discover that you don't need the fingers on the outside at all. To keep the openings from stretching any more, pack the clay gently inward, not folding it, but packing it together. Remember, clay is made up of particles, with water in between each one. These particles will move. Now, gather both openings, gently squeezing in.

With the two remaining lumps, repeating what you have done before, go into some other shapes. Just play,

and see how many different things you can do when you start with the basic tube shape. Then, put these shapes aside.

Now, with the rest of the clay, which you had previously wedged, try to make a bowl about the shape of

half a sphere. Work with concentration, never losing sight of the shape you are seeing in your mind's eye. Work slowly and with care, always aware of exactly what your fingers are doing. Make the walls as thin as you can, but leave about a quarter of an inch for the bottom.

Wedge up another lump and separate it into three or four pieces. Have an idea in your mind for a different bowl shape for each piece. Carefully and slowly try to make each one, being very aware of how you are stretching the clay, packing it where necessary, smoothing it, shaping it.

When you have finished your practice sessions, line up all your pots and look at them for a long time. Look at their gestures. Everything you make will have a gesture and a personality that comes from the feelings you bring to the clay. This is what makes your pot true to

you. Whenever I watch a beginning student making a pot, I am always amazed at how individual that person's touch is, how different from another's. This individual touch is your own fingerprint in the clay. I hope you never lose this even as you continue to develop your workmanship and style.

Although traditionally the pinch pot is very limited in its range of shapes and sizes, the technique actually does allow for greater freedom and possibilities of more forms than is normally expected.

Take the shapes you have just made as well as the ones you put aside when you were just playing with small lumps. Look at them carefully and see if any of them can be combined to make a small structure. With this idea in mind:

Wedge some clay and cut it into several different-size pieces. Leave the pieces in their original shape and try to pinch out the same form. Let the form change slightly, if it must. Look at these forms without thinking of their function—they are not bowls, though one of them may

be bowl-shaped. When you have finished them, try to assemble them in different ways until you come to an assemblage that is pleasing to the eye. Let your eye tell you — try to trust your instinct. When you are assembling, ask yourself questions like: Is it too top-heavy? Too bottom-heavy? Does it look lopsided? Does it seem to be split in the middle so that the parts look totally unrelated? Is it cluttered? Do some pieces not relate at all?

If you decide on a combination that you feel works in space — is pleasing to your eye — have some fun by doing this:

Cut long strips of very thin fabric, such as gauze, about one-half inch wide and start to wind them around your sculpture tightly without obliterating the form. Wrap about three layers of fabric until the whole thing is cov-

ered and looks like one solid mass. Does its contour look any different from the clay version? What does the contour do? Does the form look full, as though the inside wanted to push out? Is the form angular, round, amorphous, pleasing, unpleasing?

So far, you have been working with small lumps of clay. I usually like to say to my students, "A pinch pot is only as large as your thumb is long enough. So if you want to make a much larger pinch pot, you will have to use your fist for a thumb and the whole palm of your hand for fingers."

First, take a wedged lump about two and a half pounds and make a bowl-shaped pinch pot using your thumb and fingers as you have been doing all along. As the bowl becomes larger, you may find your fingers are too short. Try to figure out a way to finish thinning and shaping the wall without stretching it to the point of collapse. If you feel it is necessary, use on the outside a paddle or a 1" x 4" board whose edges have been slightly rounded, and a supporting hand on the inside. Always work with an upward motion. When you are finished with this one, make another of the same size and place it upside down, rim to rim on the first pot. Connect the rims by *welding* them firmly together. Welding means pulling the clay from one part into the other and packing it so the seam disappears. Do this firmly, mixing the clay, not merely smearing it. When the two pieces are connected, take your paddle and sculpture the form, tightening it. There should be no evidence of the seam. Now you have a clay balloon, a clay form completely wrapped around space. Change the shape and direct the contour by rolling it on the table and continuing to paddle. You will find you have some control over the shape.

When your balloon has hardened slightly, you can cut out a cover from the top or cut out two oval bowls by cutting in a horizontal direction. When you open the pieces, weld the inside seams thoroughly and smooth the rims. When you have cut the cover, add three small strips of clay, welding them on the inside to hold the cover in place on the pot. They will act as a flange.

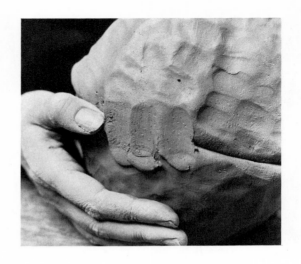

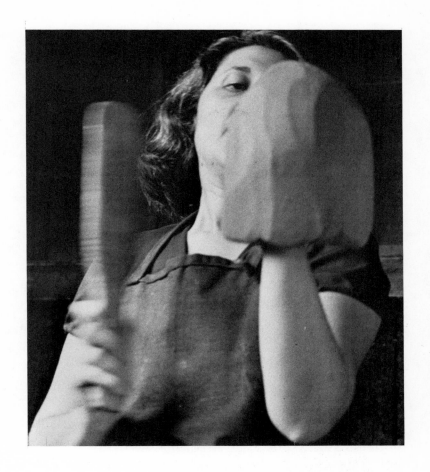

Several years ago in one of my classes I saw a student paddling a large lump of clay down over her fist. Her fist eventually tore through the lump. I became fascinated and we tried it again and again until we succeeded in keeping the upper part of the lump from tearing. This is how to do it:

Take a five-pound lump of wedged clay. Wrap your fist in cloth or a lot of plastic and push it into the lump.

Hold your fist up and start paddling on the sides of the lump, bringing the clay down over your arm. The cloth on your fist will provide a softness that will prevent your knuckles from cutting through the lump. Also, do not paddle directly on top of your fist, but on the sides, shaping the pot and directing the contour. When you are through, you can then thin the bottom of the pot with the paddle. Now take your arm out, placing the pot on its bottom.

Simple forms can also be pulled out of the clay.

Take a small lump and start to make a pinch bowl, leaving some thickness at the bottom. When you are about halfway finished, turn the bowl upside down and start to pull a foot out of the bottom. The foot itself is a tiny pinch pot. To avoid flattening the foot while the clay is still soft, hold the pot in the palm of your hand while you finish it. Let it sit on its rim for half an hour while the clay stiffens before setting it back on its foot to dry.

Take a half-pound lump and start pinching out a drinking cup. While the wall is still about one inch thick, pull some clay out to form a handle. Pull the clay slowly and gently, letting it spread outward. Let your finger perforate the handle as you give form to it. Finish shaping the wall of the pot. Make another, entirely different from the first, letting your imagination go, even to the absurd.

While you are still on the absurd, try to completely exploit the pinch method in one large, growing sculpture, welding pieces together where necessary.

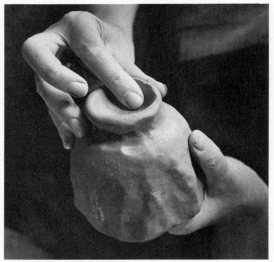

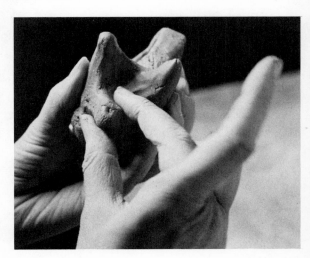

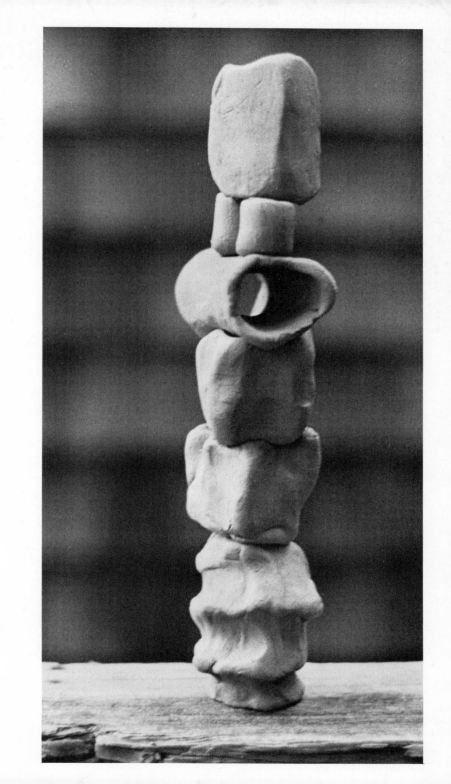

After a while, practice and doing become the same thing. It will not matter whether you are making a pinch pot or pinch-pot sculpture for practice or for keeping. The only important thing will be that you do it well, with craftsmanship, carefully considering the contour, the design, the effect the whole has on your eye. You will surely begin to develop discipline if each time you start to make a pot, you give it your full attention, concentrating as deeply as you know how on the form you are taking out of the clay, not thinking of the end or the beginning, but experiencing the very moment of every pressure and pull of your fingers as they draw up the pot. Discipline is developed in the care you take in making the simplest pinch bowl, in getting the relationship between height and width just right—pleasing to your eye and appropriate to its function. I have sometimes seen a pot that looked as though either its bottom wanted to continue beyond the table on which it was sitting or its rim had been truncated. These are the things to think about when you design a pot.

Coil

Coils have always been used as a means of building up a pot. The pinch pot is made out of one piece of clay, while the coil pot is built up out of many pieces. In this method, ropes of clay are wound around a base and welded together, smoothed out, and paddled, erasing all traces of coil. In Japan, very large pots were made by first throwing a base on the potter's wheel. When the base had sufficiently stiffened, the rest of the pot was continued in stages by building it up with coils and

smoothing the coiled part by pulling up the wall as the wheel turned.

When I first started to make large coil pots, I couldn't help feeling like a bricklayer building a house or putting up a wall. The process seemed so similar to bricklaying, except the bricks I was using were long, round and soft. As I continued to work with this method, I started to wonder why coils had to be round. I began to make fatter coils, flattening them into ribbons about two inches wide. This made building faster. Often, I use a method of building I learned in art school when a visiting sculptor from Greece was invited to spend the school year teaching the senior sculptors. He worked in wax as well as in clay, very quickly building the walls of his sculpture with large pinches of clay or wax firmly welded onto each other. He was able to build very large or very small sculptures with this method. The size of the pinches of clay was determined by the size of the sculpture.

As you learn the coil method and do a lot of work in it, I am sure you will eventually develop your own way of handling the clay. Learning a method is only a way of getting to where you want to go. The coil method is not confined to making small pots but can be useful even for building a house. You will find as you do the following exercises that your ideas will have freer expression, because with coils there is almost no end to what you can make.

Have several lumps of clay ready for the following exercises.

Take any size piece of clay out of a lump and flatten it to about a quarter of an inch with the heel of your

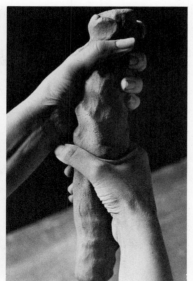

hand. Cut a circle out of it, by eye, about four or five inches in diameter. This will be the base. Take another piece of clay large enough to fill your hand and start to squeeze it into a long rope. When you are squeezing, be especially aware of how hard you are squeezing at different points. It is very easy to end up with a rope too thin in one part. Your hands are a part of you. Know what you are doing with them.

Now you can thin and smooth the coil by rolling it on the table. In rolling, your hands should roll and move out toward the ends at the same time. If you press down too hard, the coil will flatten. Weld one end thoroughly onto the base and wind the rest of the coil around the rim of the base. You should end up with perhaps two or three levels of coil. Starting on the inside, thoroughly

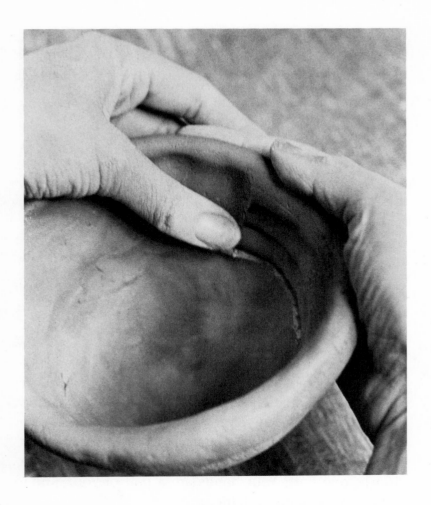

weld the levels of coil downward into the base with
your thumb, while the other hand supports the wall on
the outside. If you do not support the wall with your
hand, the pressure of welding is likely to stretch and
eventually collapse it. In the same way, weld the outside while you support the inside wall. Roll out another
coil and weld that onto the first. Before you go on,

paddle the wall and the rim, strengthening and directing the contour. Support the impact of the paddle with your hand on the inside wall. Continue building in this way, going as high as you dare.

Perhaps you have already thought: why start with a flat base? Why not start with a pinch pot and continue the rest of the pot with coils?

 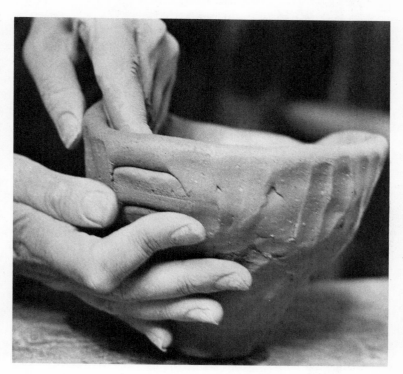

Try to make a bottle shape with this method. After you have made the pinch-pot base, be sure to let it dry for

Slip: clay suspended in water, forming a creamy, soft mixture.

one or two hours so that the rim will be able to support the weight of the coils. When you are adding the soft coil onto a slightly harder rim, it is important to score the top of the rim with a fettling knife and apply a little bit of *Slip*. Scoring opens the clay and slip lubricates it. When you place the coil on the rim, press it firmly into the scorings and weld. Paddling will insure the locking between the coil and the scorings.

If you want the shape of the pot to go out in the middle, then in again at the shoulder and neck, the coils must follow that contour. That is, if the form points outward, then each coil must be placed slightly outward. And when the form wants to start moving inward toward a neck, each coil must be placed going in an inward direction. If the clay is too soft, the shoulder may start to sag. Let the pot stiffen for an hour before continuing.

This is a good time to start a notebook of your ideas if you haven't already done so. Get into the habit of drawing your ideas of pots you want to make or pots that may fascinate you. It may be months or even a year before you act on any of your drawings, but it is important to record an idea when it comes to you. The drawing may even seem absurd to you at the time. In a month or more, when you look at it again, you will see it with a fresh eye, and you may be motivated to work on it. Draw your ideas; write your ideas.

Start your notebook right now. Draw whatever kind of pot comes into your head without worrying whether or not you can draw well. These drawings are not going to be on exhibition. They are most important in what

they say to you. Draw slowly. For a moment, close your eyes and try to see the pot you want. Imagine touching, running your finger along the edge, all around the pot. Then draw the shape you imagine. Do this with every pot you think of, concentrating on its shape, even drawing with your eyes shut to keep the image before you. If you continue to do this, drawing your ideas will soon become second nature to you.

Choose one of your drawings for the next exercise.

Start with a flat base. Pinch a piece of clay off one of your lumps and weld it onto the edge of the base. The welding can be done with one hand by pushing the piece firmly onto the base and welding downward with the thumb on the inside. The fingers on the outside support and weld the outside seam at the same time. Finish the first row, welding the vertical seams as well. Start the next row in the same way, concentrating on the welding rhythm of the thumb pushing downward on the inside and the fingers welding upward on the outside. At the same time, you should be always aware of the shape of your pot, letting your fingers work in the direction of the contour. The way you sense the shape of the pot is the way your fingers must go. If you feel the pot goes outward, then your hands go outward. We talked earlier about the gesture of a pot—let your hand be this gesture, and the clay will follow. If you feel the shape, whether it be fat, round, tall, narrow, squat, your hands will follow your sensation of that form. Throughout your work, remember always to look for a sense of the form you are working on. It is this sense, or feeling, that can make your pot lively.

I'm sure you are now beginning to see that you can build quite large with the coil method. This is the time to try it. I usually encourage my beginning as well as advanced students to work large very early in their training, to learn the feel of lots of clay in their hands and to know that they can handle it. It is easy to think that because you are a beginner, you are not skilled enough to manage a medium to large pot. If you concentrate on applying the principles you are learning and respect the limits of your medium (remember the earlier discussion on the limits of clay), I see no reason why you cannot think in terms of larger pots and build them. If I am going to make a large coil pot, I usually like to use what I call ribbon coils.

Think of a pot, or a simple sculptured form, at least eighteen inches high and whatever width your design calls for. First make some drawings of ideas, then decide which you will work on. Make a low pinch pot as a base. If you prefer to start with a slab as a base, do so. Take a large piece of clay and squeeze a fat rope out of it, about three inches in diameter. Roll it on the table, smoothing the coil without thinning it. Then, either with your hand or a stick, paddle it into a long slab about half an inch thick. The ribbon will be three to four inches wide. Weld it firmly onto your base. Because the coils are in slab shapes, each level must be applied separately. Continue building the pot, welding each level firmly onto the previous one. As your pot grows, you may find you will have to let the wall harden slightly before you can continue without collapsing it. At every second or third level, paddle the outside, guiding the shape and tightening the contour. It would be very helpful to work

in front of a mirror, to look at the pot through the mirror while shaping the contour. Since the mirror image is not the image itself, you will be able to see flaws more quickly. Also, when working on a large piece—and this goes for smaller pieces as well—you should frequently step back, even to the other side of the room, to get a fresh look at the whole pot. This long-distance view will show you if the proportions are right, if the contour is doing what you want it to do, and if there is any sagging taking place anywhere. The long-range view is an essential guide.

So far, you have used coils as a means to an end. They can also be used as an end in themselves. One day in one of my handbuilding sessions, a student was making a planter out of coils, leaving the coils on the outside wall unwelded. She discovered for herself that first, she liked the design of the exposed coils and second, it was sound to build a clay wall in this way as long as the inside wall was firmly and thoroughly welded. In allowing herself to trust her eye, she also allowed herself to find a way of working with clay that was new and exciting to her. Sometimes I like to say to my class, "Let the clay talk to you." The student with the planter did just that.

In the next few lessons you will have the opportunity to explore further the use of the coil as a surface design.

Think of a pot you would like to have on which you show the horizontal pattern of the unwelded coils. Build it.

Why do the coils have to be long and applied horizontally? Think about this question for a moment.

Sit down, open your notebook, and with a piece of soft charcoal or a brush and ink let your hand wander

3" x 3" porcelain covered pot by Nadine Hurst, Arlington, Massachusetts, showing that coils can be used in the most delicate possible way.

aimlessly along the page. Imagine, as you do this, that you have an endless coil coming out of your hand, and that you are drawing with it. Spiral it, cut it, curl it, dent it, wave it, pile one coil on top of another. Now do the same things with an actual coil. What ideas does this evoke? Jot them down before you forget them. Take one of your ideas and build it. Build it very large or very small. In this pot, all of your welding will take place on the inside wall. Be sure that as you weld, you support the wall on the outside with your other hand. If you build very large, then build as large as the kiln in which it will be fired. If you build very small, build as small as the clay will allow. Keep your clay soft.

In allowing the coils to be the surface decoration, it can be very exciting to start thinking in terms of combining different color clays in one pot. Find out from your suppliers how many clay bodies they stock, what colors they fire to, and at what temperatures they mature in the kiln. Purchase about ten pounds of each color and start experimenting.

Limit yourself to two colors and design a pot thinking of using the two colors as though you were going to paint them on a canvas. Let the canvas grow spontaneously at first until you see a certain design motif emerge that you can then direct in a more controlled way. After welding the coils together on the inside, weld a thin coat of the dark clay onto the inside wall for a clean, finished look. Now, try combining more colors into one pot.

As you work more and more in this method, I am sure you will develop your own personal way of expanding the technique.
Tele Bjork of the Mill-Race Pottery at the Old Schwamb Mill in Arlington, Massachusetts, makes use of coils by pressing them into a mold, such as a box or a plaster shape. Here is how she describes her technique:

"Instead of covering the clay with color in the form of a glaze, I add coloring oxides to the clay body itself and then build my pieces with coils and balls of various colors. I've been using our regular light brown stoneware, which is quite coarse, for some time, and recently

Reduction: a firing during which the oxygen in the kiln is reduced so that the free carbon that comes out of the air combines with the oxides in the clay body and the glazes. When this happens, the color of the metallic oxides is changed.

Oxidation: firing a kiln in which there is plenty of oxygen, such as an electric kiln.

Bisque-firing: the first firing to harden the clay before glaze-firing.

I've started also using a smooth white stoneware body, which gives somewhat more brilliant colors.

"To the two clay bodies I add a variety of coloring oxides, such as iron, cobalt, chrome, rutile, and copper [see Part Two]. I find that the range of resultant color is quite large. I've been firing only in *reduction* so far, but I'm interested in doing some in *oxidation.*

"One of the reasons I like to work with clay in this way is that I feel a continuity between the soft clay and the finished product. I've always liked pieces best when they were wet and plastic. Somehow they were always disappointing after the *bisque-firing.* The hard pink bisqueware I would cover with a coat of glaze seemed to me to be too unrelated to my experience of shaping it. When I started working as I am now, I was pleased to see that when bisqued, the pieces still seemed claylike and fluid, and I liked the pastel colors. I like the fact that the material looks like clay.

"It's very clear that the shapes of these soft balls and coils have been changed by being squeezed up against each other. In many different colors, it still looks like clay. You can put a very dark blue of one clay body against a very dark blue of another clay body and have a difference only in texture—a shiny surface and a rough surface. On some of my pieces there are two blacks together that are almost identical, but one has cobalt and iron and the other has just cobalt, and there really is a qualitative difference in the blackness.

"All the decisions about the clay are made while the clay is still wet. I think that's one reason students find it exciting to work with, too. It's very difficult for a student to put together a clay piece with a long-range plan in

53

mind. It really does have to be two different projects—one building and one glazing. That isn't so true as you gain experience, but the immediacy of this method makes it pleasurable.

"To color the clay, I poke finger holes in the ball of clay and pour the dry oxide into the holes. Then I usually add a little water and carefully start mixing and wedging. I used to wet the oxide first, but this is messier and some oxide remains behind in the mixing bowl. If the clay is quite wet, I just wedge in the dry oxide.

"So far I've been doing most of this in press molds—bottles from cylindrical forms, lids for casseroles from shallow bowl forms. I use cardboard forms or make my own plaster molds. Most of my pieces are a combination of handbuilding and wheel-throwing. But there are endless possibilities for handbuilding alone. You need not be confined to press molds; colored clay patterns can be made with all of the handbuilding methods.

"There has been relatively little work done with colored clay, and the possibilities for development are great. Each kiln load brings some new answers and many new questions and ideas."

Slab

Although slab pots have been associated with boxlike shapes, I like to work with a slab of clay as though it were a piece of fabric. Think of the clay in its soft state, feel softness, and your pots will say softness.

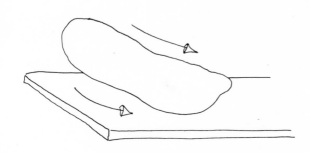

Roll out a large slab, about 15" x 15". First pound the clay lump out into a thick pancake with the heel of your

hand until it is about 12" x 12". Then lift and throw the slab down in a diagonal sliding motion. This motion will stretch the slab. Do this several times until the slab is about half an inch thick. Finally, roll the clay out with a broomstick or a long dowl two inches in diameter. As you roll out the slab, keep lifting the clay to detach it from the table. The clay will then be free to move under the rolling motion.

Tear some small random pieces out of the slab and start to make shapes with them—whatever comes into your head. Weld small pieces together, wrap them around each other, gather the clay, do whatever you need to do to complete your pot. Try to build a pot twenty-four inches high.

Tom Joanides of Cambridge, Massachusetts, often works with varied-color clays he has mixed himself. He likes to work fast and freely, using anything for a mold if he is going to press clay. The planter in the

photograph was made of small slabs of different color clays pressed into a loaf pan. It is unglazed.

Large pots and sculptures can be built with large slabs of clay as long as the form has some kind of support inside it while you are working on it. A large platter or bowl needs to be draped over anything that gives you the form you want. A closed shape needs to be wrapped around tightly crushed paper, or a foam rubber form, or bits of foam rubber. These will burn away early in the firing process.

Roll out several medium-sized slabs. Without thinking too long about what shape you are going to make, cut out a simple outline—a rectangle, oval, or random

 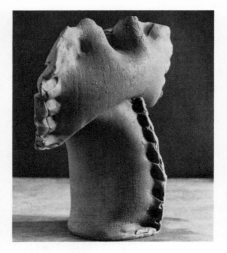 

shape. Fill it with tightly crushed paper or foam rubber and roll the slab around it. Close the seams entirely, pinching them together strongly. Let the piece stiffen for a half hour. The photograph shows coloring oxides being painted on the wet clay pieces. The oxides are cobalt (blue), copper (green), vanadium stain (yellow), and the slip of a white clay body. The piece can then be glazed with a clear glaze or left unglazed. (See Part Two.)

At this point, ideas may be coming to you about other shapes and how you would like to combine them. Work freely with your ideas or impressions without worrying too much about what the finished product will look like.

When you finally have your sculpture assembled, then you can give yourself a critique and make whatever changes you feel necessary.

Make pillow shapes. Put them together.

Make stuffed animals, stuffed people, stuffed fantasies. Make them large.

I usually like to encourage my students to build larger than they ever dared before. If your kiln is only 18" x 18" x 18" on the inside, then you can design your work in pieces, either to be arranged together, tied, or epoxied after their final firing.

Think of some large sculptural shapes. Draw them.

Saturate your vision with sculptures from art books, art magazines, and above all, museums.

When you are in the presence of a sculpture, touch it, run your hands over it, feel the sculptor's idea. And feel bigness.

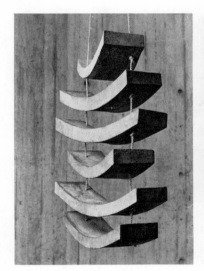 

Six swingers in unglazed stoneware with Manila rope by Marlis Schratter, Lexington, Massachusetts.

Roll out some slabs of clay and connect them by rolling them into one another, making one very large slab. Let the slab stiffen for a short period.

Design a large sculpture or functional piece, such as a

birdbath, fountain, or even a piece of furniture that will be executed in parts and put together after firing. Make drawings and little maquettes of your idea first. Then make the actual piece.

Slabs can have surface texture built into them.

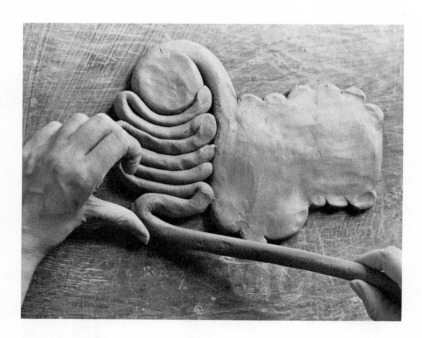 

Experiment by finding textures on which to roll slabs or which can be stamped on the slab. Some possibilities are: coarse fabric like burlap, old wood, sand, gravel, coffee grounds, and cement blocks.

Create a surface by drawing on the table with coils and connecting them by welding. Make a large slab in this way, and make a simple form with it. Remember

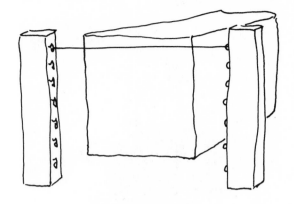

Tele Bjork's method of pressing coils into a form. Your form, in this case, is a flat table top, and your pot will be more free-form.

Slabs can also be cut out of a large brick of clay. To cut slabs of an even thickness, simply take two 2" x 4" pieces of wood about ten inches long and drive some nails into the two-inch side one-half inch apart from one another, or one-quarter inch if you prefer thinner slabs. Secure a strand of thin wire to the top two nailheads, hold the boards taut, and pull through the clay. For the next slab, lower the wire to the second set of nails.

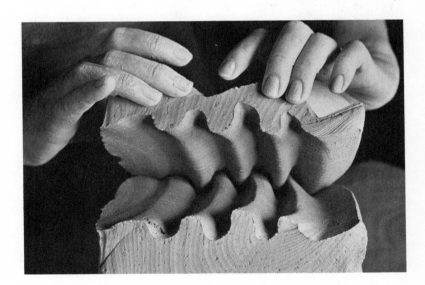

Form a large wedged lump into a brick. Have a variety of wires around — picture wire, two strands of thin wire, two strands of fairly heavy wire twisted together.

Experiment by cutting through the lump with each

wire, cutting in any direction and any number of shapes. Slabs do not have to be of uniform thickness. Quickly build a pot with the slabs you have cut.

If you want to design and build boxlike or hard-edge forms, then the clay slabs must be left to stiffen for about one day. If the weather happens to be very damp, the slabs can be left uncovered. If the atmosphere in your studio is consistently dry, lay the slabs on top of one another and cover loosely with a thin plastic sheet. The

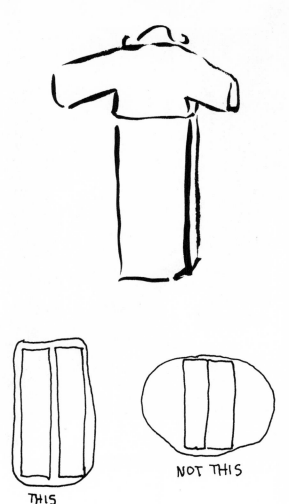

THIS   NOT THIS

greatest danger to slabs is that they may start to dry un-evenly. As the moisture leaves the clay, the particles come closer together, and the slab shrinks a little. When slabs dry unevenly, the outermost edges dry first. As the middle part starts to dry, the edges, which are already rigid, begin to curl up and crack. When I have a large platter to dry, I place it on a shelf that is made of slats and cover the rim with a collar of plastic, leaving the middle, which would be the last to dry, exposed. The slats provide better aeration. Refrigerator or oven grates are excellent as drying shelves.

Think of a large hard-edge pot you would love to build. Maybe you already have an idea in your note-book. Roll out a bunch of slabs as much in the shape of the sides of the pot as possible. For example, if your pot will be long and narrow, it would be a waste of clay to roll out circular slabs.

Cut a pattern of all the parts out of paper. When the slabs are leather-hard (test them for stiffness in the same way you did in the exercise on limits), place the pattern on them, and cut. If your pot is tall and narrow, start building it horizontally. When slabs are stiff, it is im-portant to score and slip the edges that are going to be joined. Score with a fettling knife or a sharp wood tool, and apply thick slip with a brush. Join the seams and fuse them by welding, pushing, and gentle paddling. The scorings lock and the slip provides enough clay and moisture to help the joining. To strengthen the joints, score across the inside seams, apply very little slip, and, firmly and thoroughly, weld a thin coil into them. Weld until there is no evidence of coil.

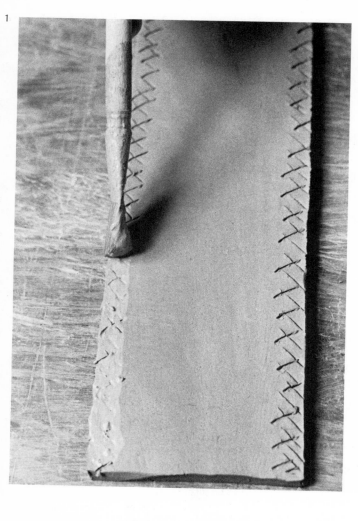

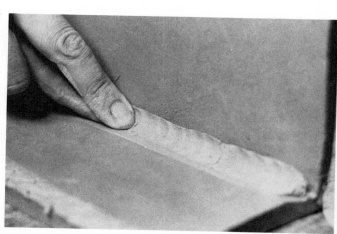

5

6

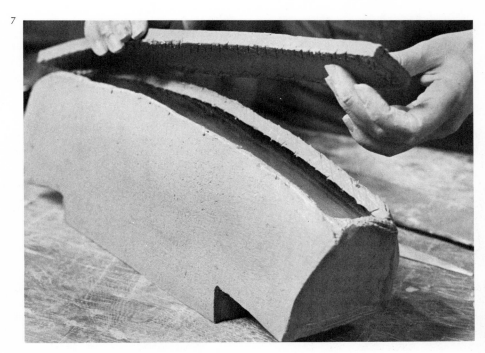

7

If your pot is going to have a cover or some kind of foot or separate stand, be sure this has been clearly planned first in your drawings.

When your pot is finished, cover it loosely with a plastic sheet to dry slowly and evenly.

Cy Lipsitt of Arlington, Massachusetts, does most of his work with slabs. One day Cy and I had a conversation about how he builds his pieces and how he developed from one way of working into another. I would like to share with you what he said:

"I first started working with a fluid, plastic kind of clay, for the purpose of doing some spontaneous things, because I was too impatient to wait for clay to cure to the leather-hard stage. So I started developing ways of working with clay to make it stay up, even though it was soft. I stuffed it with newspaper, sometimes with plastic sheets or cardboard tubes, as I did with the pants.

"Fiber-glass strands are a recent thing. I started doing some hard-edge and soft sculptures by dipping fiber-glass cloth into slip. This fuses right into the clay to create a fabric kind of texture. This was similar to burlap, but I realized that fiber glass would melt right into the clay. Regular cloth burns out and you get sort of a very brittle hollow clay form. But I wasn't too satisfied with this. I found I was just wrapping cloth around things, and I wasn't particularly happy with the results. Then shortly after that, Daniel Rhodes gave a slide lecture in which he talked about working with fiber-glass strands. I wedged them into the clay and found that there was more tensile strength in the soft plastic clay. As you

wedge them in, they crisscross with one another and they become very strong (even in the raw clay) so that you can push the clay around a lot more without breaking it. The more strands, the more difficult it is to push it around. The interesting thing is that you can really manhandle this clay. It takes a lot more strength to tear it. You can almost take a slab and walk to opposite sides of the room with it, because it is knitted together. Fiber glass melts at about 1300 to 1400 degrees and becomes a part of the clay (like putting glaze inside the clay). I found it's given me more flexibility for building large things . . . and I found that I can handle slabs without weakening them. I think fiber glass gives one much more latitude. In fact, I read recently that fiber glass is being put into roofing tar and concrete, and it isn't even being fired.

"You can have bigger slabs of clay, you can have them thicker, you can handle them better. They're still plastic. You can still meld them, bend them, twist them. They have all the quality of clay; they just stay together better. And without it, it would bend, it would flop, it would break.

"I usually carry some in my car. I give it to students who can wedge well. If they can't wedge well yet, I don't give it to them. Otherwise they end up with a clump right in the middle of the slab. Also, it's a lot harder to roll out with a rolling pin. It just doesn't move. It's not all that plastic. I spread it out . . . twenty-five pounds at a time . . . in a flattish cube and I put it on the rough side of the Masonite and I step on it to flatten it more and more . . . with work shoes. After I hurt my back, I found that rolling it was really a strain and I started doing this, because I didn't want to stop working. Once I get it down to maybe an inch and a half, I then put it on my workbench and use a rolling pin.

"Students take to it. When they are struggling with something, I say, 'Why don't you try fiber glass?' They are really amazed at the ease with which they can put things together. I feel that there's no reason why they have to suffer and struggle just because they're students. I think the worst thing that can happen to students is to run up a dark alley and have a lot of disasters. I know one woman who rolled out a huge slab and draped it inside a cardboard box, a four-sided corrugated box, with the rest hanging over. It hung there for several days. And, you know, if you took regular clay and hung it there it would have just torn. The weight would have dragged it down. She was amazed at what she did, because she knew what clay wouldn't do.

"There are limits to clay and if you can extend these limits, good. I'm all for honesty of material. Clay bends, it breaks, it shrinks, it warps, and you can capture this in the piece so that you can say that at one time it was very soft and molten. That's great. That's one thing that hard-edged clay doesn't do for you. Soft things (like the pants or the hat, even) you know must be made out of a soft material. Some of the things that I'm doing now out of the fiber glass don't show that. Some of these are going back to geometric hard-edge things. But, maybe it's because I've had this great urge to do more massive work. I was unable to because of the limitations of the material."

There are many things you can make with slabs alone, such as:

murals and wall hangings

a dinner set

a canister set

a set of stacking mugs

a teapot

covered jars

as well as many other things that may require combining all the techniques you now know, such as:

furniture

garden sculpture

a bathtub

saltcellars

toys . . .

I don't need to go on, for I hope you have long ago caught the same excitement I feel about handbuilding.

Throwing on the Wheel

Throwing on the potter's wheel can be more difficult than handbuilding because it is a physical skill that must be developed, taking time and effort to master. It becomes a total experience involving the whole body, calling on muscles that are not used every day, and requiring concentration of the kind demanded of a dancer.

I think if I were doing pottery for a hundred years I still would not lose the excitement I always feel when I watch a potter at work on the wheel. I not only see a wonderfully skilled craftsman, I see a person whose every movement is perfectly economized and in harmony with the clay and its motions.

It is simple to communicate with the clay. If you squeeze it too hard, it will tear. If you trap it while it is being centered on the wheel, it will twist (you wring its neck). If you dig your finger into it, it will gouge. If you stab it with your finger or an instrument, you will make a hole. Clay will reproduce in the negative any form

Center: to bring a wedged lump of clay into the center of the wheel.

you press against it or into it. This can be an advantage if you are working with texture and design.

A pot is like sculpture. It is a form in space, a form sitting on another form, a form hanging from another; and if the atmosphere allowed, it would be a form floating in space. Let us look at a pot, any kind of pot, forgetting its function for a while, floating in space. It becomes a form without a top or bottom. There is a hole in a part of this form and space fills the hole as though someone were inside pushing out. There is a loop and space goes through and around the loop. Get a sense of pure "thingness" of this pot, this mug, this teapot, this goblet, and become accustomed to looking at all sides, all parts, without reference to function. Then discover its function. And use it.

The way to learn to pot is to pot. You must give yourself the chance to live with clay on the wheel. Only then will the feeling that the clay and the wheel are foreign to you disappear.

When you become involved in trying to learn throwing techniques, it feels as though nothing creative is happening because you are so taken up with the repetition of each position as you try to perfect it. Each pot looks like such a failure except for one or two you then so intensely fall in love with you refuse to throw back into the clay bin. But it is in this sometimes painful, sometimes pleasurable learning process on the potter's wheel that you can really come close to yourself, to your very center.

When I was first learning to pot, I remember how the muscles ached in my back and arms and how raw the sides of my hands were from constantly scraping on the wheel head. Whenever I tried to pull the wall up between my hands I was usually so tense I would stop breathing. Centering the clay was a total mystery to me. My body was never comfortable when I tried to exert any centering pressure. Then, one day while I was watching my teacher demonstrating in class, I noticed how she leaned toward the lump, and I saw, as if for the how she leaned toward the lump, and I saw, as if for the first time, how she and her whole body related to the clay and the wheel. After this I stopped fighting with the clay, and with my new awareness I became more open to the relationship between me and a moving lump of clay.

Pottery-making is a continuous process and a continuing growing experience for the potter. Not only does one grow in skill, but within the limits that the wheel imposes, one still can find enough room in which to explore and innovate.

Sometimes I have students who just cannot wait to get on a potter's wheel and throw. I never know what their fantasies about throwing are, or if they have ever in their lives even tried it. Before I give them any instructions, I like to watch the way they approach a lump on the wheel, perhaps for the very first time.

Now I would like to encourage you to take three or four three-pound lumps of wedged clay:

Try to throw a lump whether you have ever thrown or not. Have a small bucket of water beside you with a sponge. Imagine you are a child playing, and as a child would do, simply approach this lump stuck in the middle of a revolving disk as play. Feel the clay, wet your hands from time to time. You will struggle with it for a while but try to do some of the things you have always imagined wanting to do on the wheel. Don't stop. Do the same thing with the remaining lumps.

I'm sure you felt a lot of frustration as you tried to make the images you have in your head become reality on the wheel, but I hope you also had fun with these whirling lumps in your hands.

In this section I will show you some throwing techniques but I also hope to help you to guide yourself, to discover a way to relate to the clay in motion and to increase your powers of observation. While I am showing you a technique, I want to go inside the technique with you and find out what makes it work—what the principle behind it is.

Throwing Positions

In my classes I usually have my students first go through the basic positions over and over again until they no longer forget what to do next. A simple way to do this is to learn thoroughly the first three positions—centering, making the hole, opening the floor—and then move on to the remaining positions.

If you are starting on a kick wheel, kick the flywheel with your right foot until it picks up a lot of momentum. Then start to work. Do not try to kick and work at the same time. You will develop a rhythm of kicking and working that becomes second nature.

Wedge about ten lumps and form them into mounds.

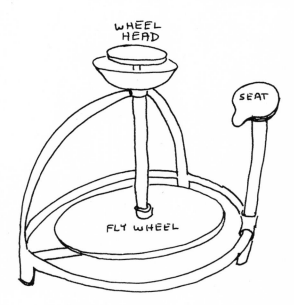

WHEEL HEAD

SEAT

FLY WHEEL

A lump large enough to fill both hands is a good size to start with. This is large enough to get you used to throwing large lumps from the start. Throw the lump hard onto the middle of the wheel and start the wheel revolving. The lump will need moisture at all times while being centered. Wet the lump with your hands and start to put pressure against it with both hands. A centered lump does not bump into you at every revolution of the wheel. When a lump is centered it means that every particle of clay is revolving concentric with every other. The force of the wheel and the thrust of your hands will push the particles into place. The clay is soft, so if you make a firm wall partway around the lump with your hands, it will bend and move within the mold your hands provide. Do not try to catch the clay — it will respond to pressure, firm and steady pressure. Not only do your hands exert pressure, but also your body behind your arms and your hands. You are leaning on the lump, not fighting with it. When I am centering, I always draw the lump up into a tall cone and bring it down into itself two or three times. This is an excellent way to give the particles room to move into a more concentric position. Wet your hands and start squeezing with both hands at the very bottom of the lump, letting the clay naturally grow upward. Then come up with the lump. You may find it more comfortable to lean your left elbow into your hip so you can push with your body while pulling with the right hand. With this position, you don't have to depend entirely on your arm muscles to do the work. When coming down, slightly tip the upper part of the cone over with cupped hands, lean your body into the clay, and come down.

1

2

3

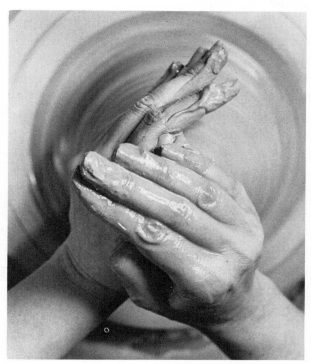

4

Notice how the clay easily gets sucked into itself. Repeat this two more times, and finish centering. From time to time, close your eyes for a moment to check if the lump is centered. You can feel a lump going into center. If it is still off-center, you will feel it moving against you, bumping into your hands. Look for this feeling. You may or may not have been able to center your first lump. Do not try to learn centering on one lump. Learn it on a hundred. After you have tried to center, go on to the next position.

With your hands still firmly on the lump and with both thumbs together as though they are glued, push down with your thumbs into the middle of the lump. With

your first two or three lumps let your thumbs reach the wheel head. This will give you a spatial feeling for where bottom will always be. In pottery it is well from the very start to find out where the limits are. Beginners' pots usually look timid because they do not let themselves find out where the bottom is, how tight a squeeze rips the clay, or how far the floor can be pulled open until the whole wall of the clay rips off and hangs like a doughnut from the hand. To open the lump, pull forward with all four fingers of the right hand in the opening. This creates the floor of the pot.

Once you have opened the floor of the pot, the next steps are raising the wall, thinning, and shaping. Here is where steadiness is important.

Add a little water to the wall of the pot. Bring your right hand around behind the lump, holding it firmly. Put the four fingers of your left hand over the right hand with your left thumb inside the pot and pressing against the inside wall. With this pressure on the wall keeping both hands steady, come up with both hands connected, bringing up the wall.

The last step will raise the wall completely. Form your right hand into a fist, then slightly bring out the index finger, making a loop with it. This hand stays on the outside of the pot while the left hand—all four fingers firmly held together—goes on the inside, facing the loop of your right-hand index finger. With pressure between the four fingers and the loop, pull up the wall. Start your pull at the very bottom and go up in one motion. This motion will be tricky for a while because the pres-

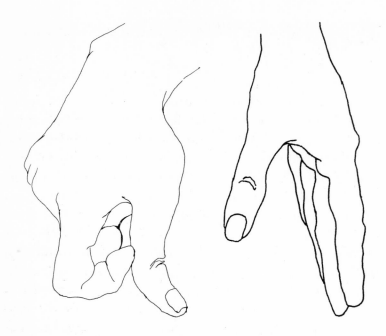

sure between the two hands varies. With every pull, trim the rim by holding it with the thumb and first finger of the left hand and hooking your right little finger over the rim.

Here are some tips:

1. Be sure your right hand is in an upright position and also leaning somewhat against the pot. That is, do not stab the clay with the knuckle of your right hand.
2. Keep the inside fingers straight and together, with the pressure in the very tips of your fingers. If they tend to spread and get pulled around, try putting a rubber band around them.

3. Keep the inside fingers firm against the pressure of the outside knuckle.

4. For support, lean your left thumb on your right hand.

5. When you are pulling a wall, concentrate on moving upward. Start the concentration even before you start to pull, being sure that you really feel upness. Your hands will soon follow.

At this point it would be best for you to repeat these positions until you feel very comfortable with them. Do not stay on one lump for more than fifteen minutes. It would be helpful if you shut out the lights and placed a small candle beside your wheel. This would create just enough light so that you could see in front of you and just enough darkness so that you would begin to rely on your sense of touch. Pot freely, without worrying what your pot looks like. While practicing in this way, keep your body relaxed (not tensed) and try to imagine you are potting out of a point somewhere in your center.

As you practice these first exercises, you will begin to realize that there are many things going on between you, the clay and the wheel. It is important to allow yourself to become aware of this interaction. For example:

1. Are your joints rigid as you work at the wheel?
2. What are your legs doing when you center?
3. What do you do to steady your limbs?
4. Do you clamp your jaw?
5. Do you hold your breath?

6. What do you feel in the core of the lump you are centering?

7. When you are bringing up the wall do you feel that you are going to make it to the top?

8. When do you reach for the water? Too many times?

You can see now how all of your body becomes involved in the act of throwing. The following exercises make you even more aware of the various parts of your body that are actively involved in the process. And the clay helps by showing you what you have done. It is important at first to become acutely aware of all your motions in order to become knowledgeable about your clay. You are learning to listen to the clay as you build a relationship with it.

Concentration

Now that you have tried a few lumps on the wheel, I suggest that you go back and deal with your problems through some concentration exercises. I feel concentration is all-important in wheel-throwing, for although throwing is a physical act, it needs all of your attention or you will not do it justice.

This exercise should take no more than ten minutes per lump. Wedge up several balls of clay about five inches in diameter. As you are working on one ball be sure to keep the other balls covered with plastic to prevent drying. I suggest that you use a timer, like an alarm clock, which — apart from making you nervous —

will keep you constantly aware of all your movements. This is not a lesson in how fast you can center or make a pot, but to show you where you are after ten minutes at the wheel. By the fifth lump you will see that you are well beyond where you were with your first pot at the end of ten minutes. In each exercise you should concentrate on something different until you are able to feel comfortable when concentrating on everything connected with your throwing at once. In this exercise concentrate on what is going on *inside* the lump. This concentration is how you become sensitive to a lump and whether it is truly centered or not. You will also discover and learn to anticipate that moment when a lump is centered, and you will begin to see that your clay does not need to be conquered. Discovery is the word. The clay will reveal its nature to you, but you must learn to listen for it.

Now throw a lump in the middle of the wheel and start to center. Concentrate on your whole body as you are squeezing the lump and bringing it up into a mound. Is your whole body providing leverage for your arms and your hands? If your answer is yes, fine; if no, take the time to find how you need to use your body to maintain the proper leverage. Then concentrate on your hands and fingers. Are your hands cutting the mound, strangling it? Are your thumbs digging a hole in the top when you don't want one? Find out what your legs and feet are doing. Adjust them if necessary for leverage.

When you are centering, think of how you would lift an infant—with firmness, using the whole of both hands, with steadiness, using your body for leverage, and with care, so you don't squeeze too tightly. Of course, the clay does not have bones in it, but like the baby it is soft and responds to firm pressure.

Continue this exercise with each lump, remembering not to stay with any lump more than ten minutes.

In this next exercise, concentrate on the floor of the pot as you open it. By this time you are getting more and more comfortable with centering the lump. You may have found that when you opened the floor of the pot, suddenly there arrived a pointed mound in the middle of the floor. This is the clay telling you that you are gouging down as you pull out the floor. As you open the floor, keep your mind on what your fingers are *really* doing and let the clay show you what you have done. Observe how far out you are pulling the floor. If you have pulled out too far, the lump will be thrown off-center and the wall will start to tear off the base.

Your concentration here will be on your hands as they come up, bringing the walls with them.

Wedge several lumps about four pounds each. Even before you start throwing, put your hands in the position of pulling up the wall. You will find you have made a clamp of your hands. With your hands in this position, go around picking up things that are moderately heavy. Notice what your fingers must do in order to be able to pick up the object. Glasses, cups and bowls are excellent for this practice. Observe the pressure your fingers must exert and *where that pressure is* in your fingers. Now go to the clay and throw each lump, concentrating on this last position and the way you exert pressure, letting the results tell you whether you have exerted

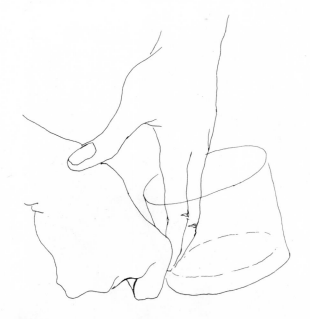

too much, too little, too uneven pressure, whether you were too unsteady or your joints too stiff. There is a lot to observe in your body in this one position alone. Allow yourself the time to do this.

Repeat the above exercise but shift your concentration to your hands in the act of coming up. In your mind's eye have the image of going up, pulling this plastic clay with you. Even say "up" to yourself with every pull.

Practice and more practice!

Cylinders

Sometimes I like to sit at my wheel and just throw several cylinders of different sizes one after another. An exercise like this is a way of pulling yourself together, for all you do is immerse yourself in the act of pulling perfectly straight, tall, thin-walled cylinders for no other reason than doing it.

Take five well-wedged lumps of two pounds, five of three pounds, five of four pounds, and five of five pounds. Start throwing with the five-pound lump, concentrating on throwing a tall, straight and narrow cylinder. Keep a ruler by your side and measure the length of every cylinder you throw. By doing this, you will be training your eye to judge the size of a pot by looking at it. You will be surprised how tall a seven-inch pot will look to you. In this exercise, concentrate on the thickness of the wall, cutting open every pot you throw.

The drawing on the next page is what a cylinder wall should look like.

Not this.

Limit yourself to four pulls for lifting the wall.

You can see how you can structure practice times for yourself using these short exercises as ways of finding out exactly what you are doing. Once you discover what you are doing wrong, you are on your way to correcting it. There are no rigid rules. Throwing is a function of your body movements, and these you will discover by observing yourself. What your body does affects the clay. You are trying to tune into a lump of clay on a turning machine. Participate with it.

Repeat the exercises with each lump of wedged clay.

After you have finished with the five-pound lumps, go to the four-pound lumps, and so on, until you reach the two-pound lumps. By the time you have reached the two-pound lumps, you surely will be throwing with more ease and your cylinders will be straighter and thinner.

Bottles

As you pot more, you will probably start developing your own concentration exercises as a way of solving problems. You will become aware of a newfound confidence and be eager to try shapes other than cylinders. Start with the bottle.

For the first few bottles, start with a tall, slightly cone-shaped pot, and then after the first or second pull, start to put some shape into the pot by exerting a gentle push with the left hand on the inside, beginning near the bottom and working up. This gives the pot its stomach. Watch what happens on the outside and guide your hand to effect the contour you desire. Do this without touching the outside. Once you have the feeling of stretching the clay on the wheel, start to throw bottles of all dimensions.

These are the phases to go through in throwing a bottle shape:

By starting to throw in a cone shape, you are anticipating the neck of the bottle and avoiding stretching it wider than the fit of your hand. From the very start in

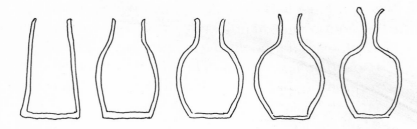

throwing, it is important to level the rim after every pull. Gently hold the rim with the thumb and index finger of the left hand, pressing down lightly with the right index finger. The pressure of the left fingers is lifting while the pressure of the right is pressing down. This will keep the rim level and designed. You will find that you can design

the rim in several ways to personal taste: a flat, straight rim, a perfectly round one, or a beveled one with sharp or soft edges. Sometimes the rim needs trimming with a needle tool. When you use the needle, do not stab but let the needle slowly cut until it goes through the wall; then lift, bringing the rim of clay with you. Now the body of the bottle must be completed before you can start to *collar* the neck. Collaring means exerting a gentle pressure on the neck, first going in and then going up with the hands. Do not put weight on the shoulder of

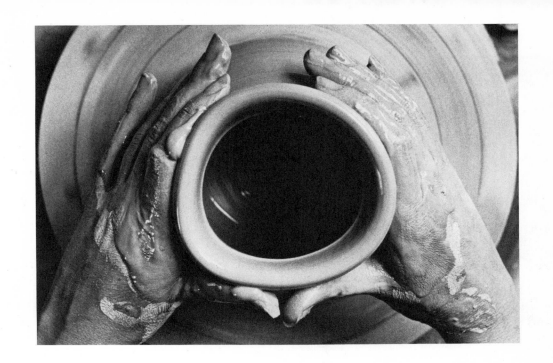

the pot or it will collapse. Squeeze gently on the neck or it will twist. As you squeeze and come up, you are pushing the particles of clay closer together. As the neck of the bottle is being narrowed, the wall becomes thicker, so it is necessary to pull the wall of the neck to thin and raise it. Since the neck is free-floating, narrow and vulnerable, you use the fingertips of both hands to pull the wall. Very often, all you need is one finger on each side of the wall. Use the very tips of your fingers to gain better control and contact. The particles can move because there is water between each one of them. However, if the clay is overworked and too watered down, the wall will become thin and soggy (tired) and start to twist and collapse.

When you have finished each bottle, trim the bottom edge with your wood tool, removing the band of excess clay. Then take your cutting wire, hold it taut down on the wheel head, and pull toward you with both hands. To take the pot off, wipe your hands and gently lift the pot, leaning it slightly onto your left hand.

Some other bottle shapes to try out:

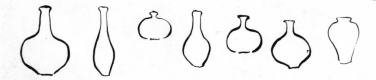

Bowls

Bowl shapes require some throwing positions different from the cylinder and bottle. From the very start, you pull the wall close to the bowl shape you want.

It is customary to throw a bowl on a plaster or wooden bat. Put a fairly thin film of slip on your wheel head and firmly place the bat on it, giving it a couple of minutes to stick to the clay. Then start to throw. If the bat should come off, put some small coils of clay on its bottom rim and the wheel head, pushing them against the bat.

When shaping the bowl, it is very important to support the outside with all the fingertips of your right hand as you apply pressure on the inside with the fingers of your left hand. Also, be sure your fingertips on the in-

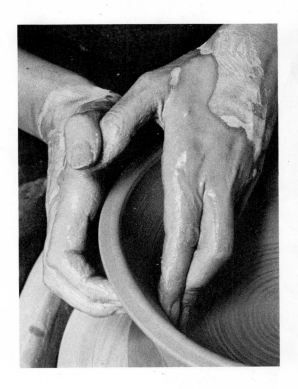

side are connecting with those on the outside. The shape of the bowl is determined by the inside shape. So, the outside hand follows the thrust of the inside hand, but also acts as support on the outside wall.

While throwing any bowl, always keep the diameter of the rim smaller than you ultimately want it. If the rim is stretched immediately to its finished diameter, it will tend to flare out and collapse before the bowl is completed. Also, the motion of the wheel constantly exerts a force on the rim, pulling it out.

Let some of your bowls dry to leather-hard for the tooling exercise (see page 97).

Although a bowl seems to be one of the easiest things

to throw, it is actually rather difficult because of the steadiness required when pulling the wall outward and the tendency of the upper wall to flop if the rim is stretched too far too soon. The shape and proportions of a bowl are also critical. The wall must come up and out without any unevenness in the inner and outer contour. The rim of a bowl is also very important. This is what gives the bowl its character. Try different kinds of rim until you are satisfied. You will find the proper rim for the kinds of bowl you end up throwing. Although you will learn in some class or from this or another book how to shape a rim, the final designing is uniquely yours, because both the perception and execution of that rim come out of you. Of course, this will be true of all your work once you are potting fluidly.

The plate is simply a low bowl.

I suggest that even between these exercises you explore other forms of all sizes, first perhaps by trying to throw an uncomfortably large pot and then immediately trying to throw a pot as little as an eggcup. Play a lot with forms, not worrying how successful they are—success will come in time. Then take one form that you love and repeat it many times, varying the height and width, finding the proportions that please you.

Pitchers

Now that you've experienced various forms, you can start thinking of designing a specific functional pot, like a pitcher. What does "pitcher" imply to you? How do you think it should look? And how do you want to use it?

Throw several shapes you feel will function as pitchers, large and small. Just as you have finished each one, before cutting it off the wheel head, shape the pouring spout. Hold the outside rim with one hand and gently stretch it with one finger of the other hand, curving the lip out and slightly down. This curve should provide easy flow for liquids.

Take the pitchers off the wheel and let them dry to a leather-hard stage.

Tooling

Sometimes pots have a little extra clay at the bottom that must be shaved off. This is called tooling, *or* turning. *Tooling can be time-consuming and many production potters design their ware to require no tooling at all. Any pot whose contour has no extended foot really does not need any tooling. Simply soften the leather-hard bottom rim with your thumb, beveling it slightly, and the pot is finished.*

As the rim of a pot is very important, so is its foot, which is uniquely designed for the pot and is determined at the time of throwing. A pot is like a sculpture in the round. It can be shown from all sides. It is only for reasons of function that a pot sits on its foot. Some pots call for a hollowed-out foot and some for a fairly flat bottom. Some pots are never tooled at all if they have been so designed and skillfully cut from the wheel head.

When the pot is leather-hard, feel the thickness of the foot with your hands to get an idea of how thick the bottom is. Then turn it upside down in the center of

the wheel head. With the wheel revolving, tap the pot with your hand a few times until it gets pulled into the center by the movement of the wheel. Another way to center it is to put the pot as much in the center as possible and hold a needle to the side of the foot as it revolves. You will get a slight incision in one side of the foot. This means the pot is still off-center. Just gently slide the pot away from the mark and check it again. Soon you will be able to judge by eye when the pot is centered. Then hold it in position with three small rolls of clay called *keys*.

Start by leveling off the bottom, beginning at the center and going out to your right. The trimming or turning tool is held in front of you at a forty-five-degree angle to the bottom and the flat edge parallel to your body. Then trim the side bottom. For a pot without a foot it is best to tool the bottom slightly concave so the pot rests on its strongest point, the bottom rim. Especially if your clay has *grog* in it, burnish or polish with a wood tool the area you have tooled to bring back the softness of handthrowing. Burnishing can also be done with your finger. This pushes in the grog and packs the clay, eliminating any harsh scratches the metal makes in tooling.

Grog: fired clay that is ground and added to wet clay. Grog reduces the shrinkage of large sculptures and slabs.

In tooling a foot on a bowl, you follow the main contour of the pot. The bowl will have a stem on the bottom that will become the foot. With the flat part of your tool, trim the outside of the stem until it is the diameter you want, then with the rounded end integrate the stem with the body so you have an unbroken line flowing from foot to body. Then hollow out the bottom until the line of the inside follows the line of the pot. Occasionally tap the bottom to see if it is getting too thin. If the sound

is hollow, it is thin enough. Think of a foot as a removable rim that is placed on a mound. Design the foot to be pleasing to the eye. Some possible foot designs:

As you work and discover your own aesthetics, you will evolve a foot design that will be suitable to your work. In the practice stage, however, concentrate on learning to tool and doing it with craftsmanship without worrying what your style is—this will emerge.

Handles

When you are working on pots that need handles attached to them, the most efficient way to work is to make the handles first, tool the pots while the handles slightly stiffen, and then apply the handles. A handle is literally pulled out of a lump of clay.

Take a medium-size lump of wedged clay and shape it into a short, fat coil. Hold the coil in one hand and with the other hand, which must always be kept wet, start to pull the clay, stretching it downward—like milking a cow. The clay will move into a long, fluid coil, which you then cut off at the wide end, curve into the shape of a handle, and place down on a bat to dry slightly. Always pull more handles than you need so

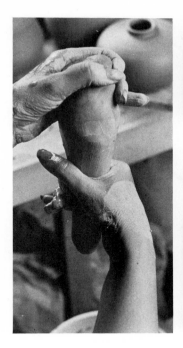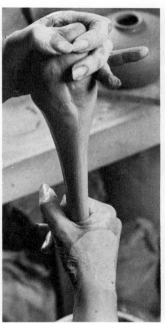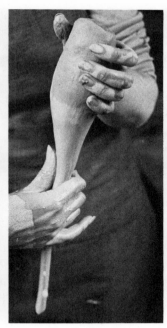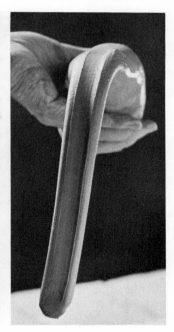

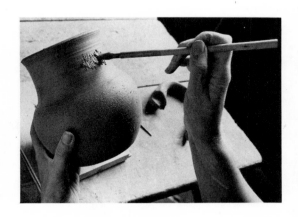

you can discard those that are not the right length. When it is time to attach the handle, look at the contour of your pot and try to determine the way the handle must grow out of the form. Score and slip the two areas on the pot where the handle will be attached and, while supporting the wall with one hand on the inside, attach the top part, welding it thoroughly. With your thumb, attach the bottom part, leaving your thumbprint if you so desire. This action may feel awkward at first and you may even drop the pot. It is best to hold the pot in a horizontal position while placing the handle. Once the handle is on, do not work on the surface of it or you will lose the fluid line that pulling gives it.

Another way to attach a handle is first to attach a very

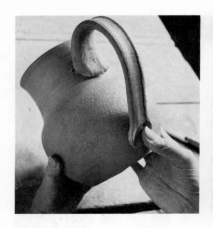

short coil onto the upper part of the pot. Hold the pot in one hand in a horizontal position with the opening facing you. Then pull the handle right out of the pot and attach the end to the lower end of the pot. This kind of handle looks as though the clay had been pulled right out of the body of the pot.

Throwing Off the Top of the Lump

Many potters like to work off the top of the lump, especially if they are making many pots of one design or pots that require more than one piece, like a set of mugs, bowls of the same size, sugars and creamers, goblets, teapots. About one dozen pots can come out of one twenty- or twenty-five-pound lump.

Wedge up as large a lump as you can. Try to center the whole lump, although it is not necessary to center it completely. You should have a cone-shaped mound. Center a small lump from the top of the mound, holding your arms steady. Do not push down into the mound.

You should have a doorknob shape on top of the lump. Make a hole, stopping at the stem part of the doorknob.

The opening position here is a little different from the one you first learned. Take two rubber bands and tie the first two fingers of your right hand together and the last two fingers together. Put the first two fingers inside the pot and the last two outside. Pull open the pot with the inside fingers, squeeze with the outside ones, and come up, bringing the wall up with you. Let your left hand help. You may find this position very awkward at first. Perhaps you can become accustomed to the position by picking things up to exercise your fingers.

In shaping the wall of the pot, use the fingertips of

both hands as you did in the bowl. When throwing small pots, I find the very tips of the fingers more sensitive and sturdier than the knuckle.

Before removing the pot, trim the bottom edge with your wood tool to tighten the bottom contour. When you cut a pot off the lump, let the wheel rotate slowly. Hold the wire loosely in both hands. Keep your right hand steady as you let your left be pulled by the motion of the wheel. The wire then comes out at your right. Practice this action on solid lumps.

After you become accustomed to the new hand positions, set yourself some practice exercises for all the pot shapes you can think of: cups, saucers, bottles, small vases, eggcups, bowls (shallow, deep), pitchers.

By now, you may be wanting to design covered pots and teapots. The lid designs for these pots vary.

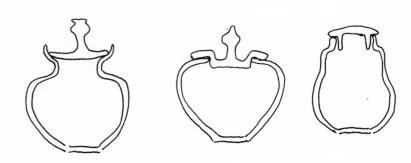

Explore one lid design at a time. I find an exercise like this exciting because of the wide range of forms I can discover when I limit myself to one kind of design.

The first lid in the drawings is the simplest because it

requires no flange. It is held by a collar in the pot. This is a pot design that can have many variations. When you've made one pot, measure halfway inside the collar with your caliper and keep that measurement for the lid. Trim the bottom and cut off. Center a small, fairly flat lump, sandwich it in your hands, and push down with your thumbs, letting a small mound emerge from the top. This mound will be the knob of your lid. Throw the flat part in a horizontal direction until you have a disk shape. Measure with the caliper and correct the size until you have the right one by cutting the excess off with a needle tool. The knob can be a tiny thrown pot, or it can be left solid and squeezed tall and narrow. Keeping your fingers very wet, take the neck of the knob between first fingers and thumbs, squeeze gently, and push slightly downward. The knob will grow upward. You will soon get a sense of how hard to squeeze without breaking the neck. You can have fun practicing this position by making solid minarets of all shapes. To remove the cover, first trim with your wood tool just under the cover, then cut with your wire.

The second lid is still thrown right side up, but will have a flange, which is the stem of the lump. The pot design for this kind of lid must have some kind of shoulder on which the collar of the lid rests. This design can also have many variations, provided there is a shoulder for the lid. Measure with your caliper where on the pot's shoulder the collar of the lid will end. The flange will fit naturally.

Again, make a disk shape, letting a knob emerge. Instead of throwing a straight horizontal disk as you did in the previous lid, lift the clay from the stem, making a little shoulder, then throw the rest of the lid in a horizontal direction. The curved part will rest on the shoulder of the pot and the stem will be the flange that fits into the pot.

To remove the cover, make a clean mark with your finger or a tool about three-quarters of an inch down the stem and cut it off with your wire. This kind of lid is really best for small pots because its flange is solid and would be too heavy on a large pot.

Both of these lid designs need only be trimmed with a fettling knife when they are leather-hard to smooth the bottoms.

The third lid is thrown upside down with the flange pointing upward. These lids can be designed from flat to dome shapes, and the pots can vary widely. The lid needs a rim on which to rest. Throw a lot of pots of

different shapes, keeping a slightly raised rim on which to set the lid. With your caliper, measure the inside of the pot's rim — this will be the setting for the flange measurement.

Center a small lump, keeping it rather flat. Make a wedge-shaped opening as though you were going to throw a shallow bowl, and throw the clay in an almost horizontal position, keeping a roll of clay on the rim. From this roll you will pull the flange. Widen the roll by slightly flattening it to a band, then push down halfway between the inner and outer rims of the band. The inner rim becomes the flange. Throw this into a wall, then measure the flange. If it is too big, gently push the rim inward. If it is way off, throw more.

When tooling the top of this lid, place it on the pot to trim. This will give you a more integrated feeling for the lines of the whole unit. If the rim of the lid extends beyond the rim of the pot, no knob is necessary. Otherwise, any kind of knob or handle can be applied separately.

Try to think of other kinds of cover or try to dream up combinations of the three you know. Stay with covered pots for a while in your practicing, making whatever combinations come into your head.

The lidded pot naturally leads to the teapot or coffee-pot.

Make some drawings of teapots you may have imagined wanting to make, and throw them. Throw at least a half dozen.

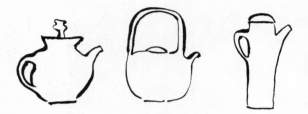

Making the spout is very much like making the neck for a bottle. Center a small lump and throw it into a narrow cylinder. Narrow the top portion even more by gently pushing inward and upward at the same time, keeping your fingers wet. Throw several—some cone-shaped, some bottle-shaped. When throwing something tall and narrow like the neck of a bottle, it is necessary to use more water than you usually do in ordinary throwing.

When you come to putting the spout and the handle on the pot, try the different spout shapes first, keeping in mind whether your handle will be a top or side handle. Look at the shape of your pot and determine

which spout flows out of it more fluidly. When the spouts are leather-hard, cut the wide ends in a diagonal direction and fit the spout to the pot. Be sure the pouring end is on a level with the rim of the pot. If the spout is put on too low, you will not be able to fill the pot without losing your tea through the spout.

Before applying the spout, pull some handles and let them set. When you have decided which spout to use, make a mark on the pot around the spout and drill about seven holes in that area with your fettling knife or

a narrow straw. Then shave away enough clay over the holes until the area is slightly concave for easy pouring. Score and slip the spout and the pot, and attach the spout firmly, welding until the seam disappears. When the pot dries, scrape the excess clay from the holes on the inside.

Set of stoneware goblets by Kathleen Ingoldsby, Arlington, Massachusetts.

Make a set of goblets. In making a set of anything, try to figure out a way that feels comfortable to you of measuring the pots so that they are the same size. Eventually you will be able to do this by eye.

Try a set of dinner plates and mugs.

Design a set of stacking canisters, mugs, or bowls.

Now that you are throwing with confidence, go back to the first shapes you tried and try to throw them large.

Start with the cylinder again. Wedge three or four ten-pound lumps and throw tall, narrow cylinders. Try

Thrown stoneware fantasy teapot with coils by Tom Joanides, Cambridge, Massachusetts.

Combined thrown and handbuilt stoneware pot by Tom Joanides.

to keep the walls thin. A larger lump requires more force, so do not be afraid to connect strongly with your clay.

Save these cylinders, no matter how awful they look to you. Throw them on plaster bats and then let them stiffen slightly. Shift your concentration back to hand-building and spontaneously combine the forms into one big pot, reshaping them, paddling them, perforating them, adding handbuilt parts, doing whatever your imagination dictates at the moment.

Design a simple project, whether functional or non-functional, in which you try to combine all or any of the handbuilding techniques with any thrown shapes.

Build it.

By this time, you have enough pots for a kiln load. If they have been drying for at least five days, they are in the greenware or raw stage. That is, they are bone-dry. You are ready to bisque-fire them. A bisque-firing is preliminary to the glaze-firing. Although the pots you will put into the bisque-firing are dry to the touch, the clay still contains some moisture and must be fired very slowly in the first stages to avoid exploding. Sometimes I become extra cautious, especially if I am firing large sculptures. I leave the kiln cover open overnight with the switches on low to allow free and slow escape for the moisture. If I am firing the gas kiln, I leave the pilots on overnight. At about 300 or 400 degrees Fahrenheit, the clay loses what is called its atmospheric moisture, or the rest of the dampness you cannot see in the greenware. At about 1000 degrees, the clay loses its chemical water and begins to shrink. The bisque-firing ends at about 1900 degrees. Once pots are bisqued, they are safe to handle in the glazing process because the clay has become hard enough to handle without shattering easily, yet still very porous, so the glaze will adhere.

part

2

Raw Materials	Approximate Amounts in Pounds
Feldspar	10
Cornwall Stone	10
Whiting	10
English China Clay	10
Magnesium Carbonate	2
Barium Carbonate	2
Flint (Silica)	5
Albany Slip	10
Zircopax	1

Coloring Oxides	Approximate Amounts in Pounds
Red Iron Oxide	2
Cobalt Oxide	½
Copper Oxide	½
Manganese Carbonate	1
Rutile	2
Granular Rutile	2
Granular Ilmenite	2
Granular Manganese	1
Yellow Ochre	½
Vanadium Stain	½
Nickle Oxide	½

Glazing

Even while you are planning what you are going to make, you should have color and texture in mind. The glaze, which is the surface of the form, must be thought out in terms of the form. A glaze is the finishing touch to a pot. Even to decide not to glaze a pot or to glaze only a small part of it is thinking in terms of its form. A very exciting thing to do is to project slides of paintings—modern, landscape, even some Rembrandt drawings, etc.—onto unglazed pots and observe how the canvases seem to wrap themselves around the form, how some paintings fit the form and others do not. Then make lots of designs, maybe starting with simple brushstrokes on a light vellum paper and then cutting the paper to fit into a slide frame. Project these different parts onto your bisque pots. This will begin to give you a good sense of your own feelings about design and will be a way of finding out about your ideas of surface decoration in relation to the forms you have been developing.

POUND SCALE

GRAM SCALE

SIEVE

GLAZE
BUCKETS

BASINS

INSECT SPRAY

WAX
RESIST

SPONGES

SPATULAS

An excellent way to develop a sense of form and color is to visit museums. Saturate yourself with whatever pottery collection your museum has. Spend a couple of hours observing pottery forms (china and porcelain as well). Another day study only pottery decoration. Then try to find someplace that shows or sells contemporary pottery and compare these contemporary statements with what you saw in museums.

It is not such a simple matter to design the glaze for a pot. Sometimes all of the glazing decisions are made at the time you are working on a pot, or even before you wedge your clay. And sometimes you can wait until the pot is bisqued, when its shape and character then reveal to you a certain treatment. But this happens when you are familiar enough with your glazes so that you know what the fired result will be.

You are probably thinking about, or are in the process of, setting up a space for your studio and maybe you have taken some pottery courses with several glazes already at your disposal. Whether you are working in the classroom or your own space, you should be systematic in your approach to glazing. That is, you decide at the time you are going to glaze which glazes you are going to use, and you know what temperature glazes to use because you've been working with a stoneware body.

It is best to start with a palette, perhaps white, black, gray, or white matte and Albany slip, which is a dark shiny brown when fired above 2200 degrees Fahrenheit. Once you have decided on your glazes, you have in one sense limited yourself. On the other hand, you have allowed yourself a specific range within which to exploit many glazing and designing possibilities.

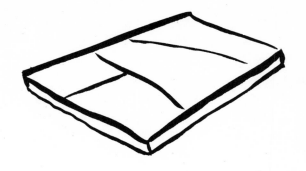

If you have access to glazes, choose two or three, like a white matte, a black matte and a brown matte. To begin with, either find out if these glazes will fuse together when overlapped or make some tests overlapping them on a test tile about 4" x 4". If you do not have access to any glazes, start with this formula, which is a glaze my first teacher gave me when I started to do pottery:

Cornwall Matte C/7-10*

Cornwall Stone	50
Whiting	20
English China Clay	20
Zinc Oxide	10
	100

STIFF BRUSH

To mix ten pounds of this glaze, use five pounds of Cornwall stone, two pounds Whiting, two pounds English china clay, and one pound zinc oxide. For a five-pound batch, just halve each weight. Stir the dry mix thoroughly and pour it into about two quarts of water. Let the glaze become saturated with the water for about twenty minutes, then mix either with an electric mixer or a large rubber spatula. Add water gradually if the glaze is too thick. It should be the consistency of heavy cream. If you make the glaze too watery, let it settle for a few hours and then pour the top water out.

A good way to test a glaze for proper thickness is to put your fingers in the mixture. If the glaze adheres to your fingers and fingernails while still showing the outline of your cuticles, then it is the proper consistency.

The glaze may be a little lumpy. Before you use it,

Indicates cone number. Refer to the temperature chart at the back of this section.

pour it through a fine-mesh sieve or very fine screen. This fully mixes the glaze. It is good practice to sieve your glazes each time before you use them. Add a handful of *Epsom salts* to your glazes to keep them suspended and easily mixable.

Epsom salts: magnesium sulfate.

Mix up a five-pound batch of Albany slip, sieving it as you did the Cornwall matte. Albany slip fuses with the Cornwall matte to give a varied light-brown khaki satin matte.

Albany slip becomes black when cobalt oxide or copper carbonate is added to it. These mixtures can work beautifully either under or over a white glaze. To get a very shiny black, add five percent cobalt oxide. To get a gunmetal black, add twelve percent copper carbonate.

The percentages of coloring oxides added to a glaze are usually figured on the hundred-gram, pound or ton batch. That is, if you start out with a hundred grams of glaze and to it will be added five percent of an oxide, add five grams to the hundred grams. If you weigh out two thousand grams of Albany slip, which is twenty times one hundred, add twenty times five grams of cobalt, or one hundred grams, to the batch. For the copper mixture, add twenty times twelve grams, or two hundred and forty grams of copper to two thousand grams.

When these mixtures fuse with a white matte, the cobalt batch turns gray-blue with some areas of brighter blue, the copper batch turns a greenish khaki and the straight Albany slip turns a soft brownish khaki. As you experiment with these, you will notice that the thickness of glaze affects the colors. Always, however, keep the

AT A SLANT

INTO THE HANDLE

MOVING WITH
THE FORM

ON BEVEL OF
DEEP FOOT

ALMOST HALF WAY UP

Albany slip very slightly thinner than the glaze. If the Albany slip is too thick, it will crawl away into blotches in the firing.

Because stoneware pots are fired flat on the kiln floor and shelves, it is very important to keep the bottoms of all pots completely free of glaze. Potters use a wax emulsion, which your supplier will have, or else you can heat two-thirds paraffin and one-third beeswax in a wide double boiler or an electric frypan. The bottoms of the pots are dipped into the wax and allowed to dry. The best way to cover the bottom of a pot is to dip about one-eighth to one-fourth inch up the side as well. Then, if the glaze melts down the side in the firing, it will not reach the bottom and adhere to the kiln floor. You may find that you want much more of the clay body showing, so you dip the bottom well into the wax, up to one or two inches. The decision to do this, of course, depends on the form and the kind of glaze you wish to use.

Some ways of waxing a foot:

wax applied at a slant

wax applied into a handle

wax on the bevel of a deep foot

wax almost halfway up

Applying the Glaze

The easiest and most convenient way to glaze is to dip the pot. The inside of the pot is always glazed first, so if some glaze dribbles on the outside you can easily sponge it clean again.

First quickly rinse the pot in clean water to get rid of any dust. Then pour some glaze into the pot and quickly pour it out, turning the pot as you pour, allowing the glaze to cover the whole inside. If the pot is small, put your hand in it and spread your fingers, holding the pot by the force of your fingers, and dip it up to its rim. If the pot is too large for the fingers of one hand to support, use the pressure of both hands on the inside. When the glaze dries, dip the pot upside down, finishing the rim. After glazing, *always sponge-wipe the bottom of the pot thoroughly.*

When you use two or more glazes, you open yourself to many possibilities of application. The inside of a pot can be one glaze, and the outside another. This is a very straightforward application. Once the inside of a pot is glazed, the outside can be dipped so the glaze forms vertical stripes.

Dip the pot horizontally without letting any of the glaze run into the inside. Then dip the other side into another color (the Albany slip, perhaps), overlapping the first glaze somewhat. If your pot is round, then the dipping will produce circular shapes. The shape of the pot determines the path the glaze will take. The overlapping of the white and the Albany slip will give a light-brown khaki color.

If you want both the inside and the outside of the pot to have stripes:

hold the pot by the rim and the foot and dip it two-thirds

of the way into the glaze, glazing both sides in one stroke. Then do the same with the other glaze, overlapping the first color.

To achieve a horizontal or slightly diagonal direction in the design,

simply dip the pot right side up in one glaze and upside down in the other, overlapping the first glaze. Remember to glaze the inside first.

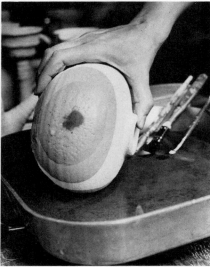

I'm introducing wax resist at this point in the glazing discussion because I feel it is important to see wax as one of your color potentials. Wax acts as a stencil. That is, it protects either the clay body or the glaze from being covered with another glaze. The wax, then, is used just as the glaze is.

If you want to preserve some of the shiny brown of the Albany slip, dip part of the brown area into the wax or paint a design on the Albany slip. When the wax has thoroughly dried, dip the whole pot in the white glaze. Wherever there is wax, the glaze will be shiny brown, wherever the glazes overlap, light-brown khaki, and where there is no brown, it will be white.

Pouring a glaze is convenient when the glaze bucket

is not full enough for dipping or when the pot is too big for the bucket. It is also another valid way to glaze. When you pour, you can direct the pour of the glaze around the pot. As you do this, imagine the pouring container is a huge brush with which you are applying lots of glaze. When you pour, you must pour abundantly, unless you want little dribbles, so the glaze (as it falls) bathes the whole side of the pot.

Hold the pot upside down, being certain that your hand is not going to be in the line of pouring, lean the lip of the container against the side of the foot of the pot, and pour as you turn the pot almost a full circle. I suggest you try this movement without glaze first, to give you the feeling of fluid movement. Practice it as many times as you need to. Also, try actually pouring with water on any bowl in your kitchen so you can learn how to direct the pour. Two or more glazes can be poured in this way to overlap.

When the pot is too large and heavy or awkward to hold with one hand, set it upside down on two sticks over a large basin and pour all around the side. And if you don't have a basin large enough for the pot, simply lay out a very clean plastic cover cloth, sit the pot in the middle of it on two sticks, and glaze the pot. When you are able to remove the pot from the plastic, you can then pour the glaze back into its bucket. Then the rim of the pot can be retouched with a brush. When applying glaze with a brush, flow the glaze on one stroke at a time, not scrubbing with the brush, but in one fluid motion.

Applying glaze with a brush is useful when you are

133

Wall hanging in terra-cotta with low-fire glazes by Jane Ulrich, Northampton, Massachusetts, showing how high one can fly in fantasy.

working with a design requiring brush techniques or when you are using low-fire commercially prepared bottled glazes in the temperature range of about 1700 to 2000 degrees Fahrenheit. These glazes are specially prepared and are made to be used only with a brush. It is best to follow the glazing directions given on the bottle.

When you are using a brush, you must be sure that you either apply three coats of glaze (three coats equals one pouring or dipping) or use thicker glaze. You can either have separate small buckets containing glazes for brushing only, or, before you stir your glaze, while it is still settled, siphon the water off the top, save it, and use the glaze in its thicker state. The consistency of this glaze should be about the same as that of hot melted chocolate.

Have different-size brushes in your glaze repertoire— round Japanese brushes, painting brushes from the hardware store and a few flat, sable paint brushes from an art-supply store. For special effects, I have even made a brush by taking a bunch of soft paper towels, rolling them loosely together, and cutting long strips in the wad. This makeshift brush can be especially useful in applying broad wax designs. If whatever you innovate works for you, then it is right. This is all part of finding your way into a creative working rhythm.

When you start thinking about painting on a pot, go back to the little slide show we discussed earlier. Start to consider painting on a pot in broad, free strokes. Practice this technique with coloring oxides and wax on paper first. Another way both to practice and experiment is to have some slabs of bisque clay available to

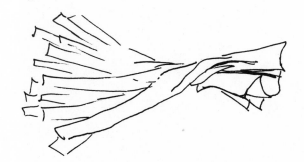

use as though they were a canvas. Later these will serve as a reference. After you have done a few of these, it will become clearer to you how to think of the whole design and have it be spontaneous at the same time.

Coloring oxides, *such as iron, cobalt, copper, can be applied over white or light glazes in the same way that glazes are applied. When they are applied to the surface of a glaze, they will* fuse *with the glaze and color it.*

Glaze some pots in the white matte. Prepare the coloring oxides cobalt and iron by mixing them each with water until they are watery. Try them out on paper first to be sure of the mixture. If most of the paper shows through the brushstroke, the mixture is too watery. If the mixture looks like glaze, it is too thick. Think of some of your practice strokes, and then apply them to the pots. The oxides can be applied over one another or in combination with wax resist. Also, try mixing some of the oxides. For example: one part cobalt oxide and three parts copper carbonate, two parts cobalt and one part manganese dioxide, seven parts vanadium stain and one part cobalt oxide, etc. If you get stuck, go back to paper and do some more experimenting. Try anything you can think of.

Another brush method for applying coloring oxides onto the glaze is what I like to call flinging. This can be done delicately with a small, long-haired brush or with great vigor with a very large brush. When I glaze this way, I practice many times on paper before I approach the pot. It is such a spontaneous method that I feel I want to build up a rhythm in my hand motion.

Practicing this method will also help you determine how much oxide to have on your brush for the size and look of the design.

Hold the pot in one hand, or place it on a stand at a small distance from you, maybe ten inches. Saturate your brush with oxide and fling with a forceful movement of your wrist, letting the oxide fly off the brush onto the pot. Practice this many times on paper also. It will show you how you can control the force of the fling.

Spraying oxides on a glaze is a way of coloring the whole glaze surface. When you spray, you can control the darks and lights of the color.

Start with a pot with white matte on it. Paint or fling a design on it with wax. When the wax has dried, spray the oxide on the pot.

Wax resist can be used with the sgraffito technique as well. Sgraffito is the technique of scratching away slip or glaze to reveal the color of the clay body underneath. It is a technique that allows you to draw fine lines. If you want to fill in what has been scratched away with another glaze or coloring oxide, then you will have to use wax to protect the glazed body.

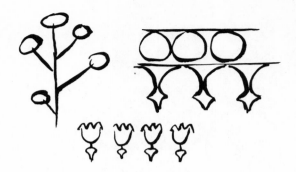

First, decide the color glaze you want for the whole pot and which one you want for the sgraffito design. Apply the first glaze onto a bisque pot, then cover with wax the areas where there will be a design. Flow the wax on with single strokes, being careful not to take the glaze with you. Then think carefully about a design, one from your notebook perhaps. Plan out your design on the wax surface with a felt-tip pencil first, then scratch through both the wax and the glaze under it with a needle tool. When all the desired areas have been cleared of wax and glaze, simply apply the second glaze by dipping, pouring, or brushing it over the wax and onto the revealed areas. If any drops of glaze adhere to the wax (be sure the wax is dry before you start to draw) remove them if you wish with a damp sponge. If you use a commercial wax and thin it down with water, say three-quarters wax, one-quarter water, the wax will not chip and peel off as you draw through it. The bottle in the photograph was done in this way. First the white glaze was applied, then the wax wherever the design was going to be. The dark part was what was scratched away and dipped in dark-green glaze. The cup and saucer have clay exposed in the design as well. One of the beautiful results of using the wax-resist technique is the occasional specks of glaze left on the wax that will, of course, remain on the design after firing. It is part of the soft-edge look of wax-resist glazing.

Paper resist *is another very useful way of achieving broad, simple designs. The principle is the same as that of wax resist. Whatever area on the glazed pot you wish to preserve is covered with a soft, not too absorbent,*

Stoneware bottle, cup and saucer by Nancy Freeman, Newton, Massachusetts, showing the use of wax in sgraffito.

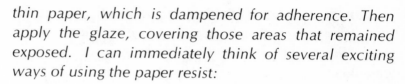

thin paper, which is dampened for adherence. Then apply the glaze, covering those areas that remained exposed. I can immediately think of several exciting ways of using the paper resist:

Cut a large, simple shape and apply it to the pot. For example, a freehand circle.

Try cutting out a spiral and putting it inside a shallow bowl.

Cut a simple design and put the positive onto the pot. If a free brushstroke is called for in your design, use wax.

Slips

Glazing and decorating do not always happen after a pot is bisqued. Many potters make extensive use of slips, which are applied to a wet pot—many times even before the thrown pot is taken off the wheel. Slips can be made from your own clay by taking some of the slip from your slip bucket, adding enough water so that it is very thick and creamy, and sieving it through an eighty-mesh sieve or very fine screening. Then add the coloring oxide and about five percent Zircopax to lighten the clay, and sieve the whole mixture again. If it is too liquid, let it set for a while until it thickens.

The proportion of coloring oxides to slip is something you must find for yourself by experimenting on leather-hard slabs.

You might start with three parts liquid iron oxide to one part slip, one part oxide to one part slip, and one part oxide to three parts slip. Also try equal amounts of iron oxide with cobalt oxide and add this mixture to the slip. After these test slabs have been bisque-fired, simply glaze them with a thin coat of your white matte or clear glaze.

Also, experiment with the slips of other clay bodies, like porcelain, for example. Check the clay bodies your supplier carries and try their slips on the body you are using. Even take the slips of the low-fire bodies and test them on your clay at a high temperature.

An engobe is a slip made up mostly of ball clay and kaolin with a small amount of feldspar and sometimes other fluxes, and silica, which lends hardness to the slip. Coloring oxides are added dry to the engobe formula in the same way that glazes are made up with coloring oxides in them. Engobes can be made to fit moist pots, greenware or bisqueware. If you are going to use an engobe on greenware and bisque pots, then it needs extra kaolin to reduce its shrinkage and to fit the dry clay body, which has already undergone some shrinkage. An engobe for dry clay is closer to a glaze in its composition than one for wet clay.

Try some experiments.

Start by taking equal amounts of kaolin and ball clay, perhaps forty grams of each, fifteen to eighteen grams of silica and two to five grams of feldspar. Apply this to a leather-hard slab of your clay body. Then fire and glaze with a clear glaze over it. Then vary the amounts of silica and feldspar, perhaps bringing them to a more equal amount, say fifteen grams of each. This will lend more melt to the slip and fit more closely with the glaze. Try lowering the clay content slightly.

Flux: a glaze ingredient that lowers the melting point of the glaze.

Glazes

Clay and glazes are more or less made up of the same compounds—basic, neutral, and acidic oxides, with fire (heat) as their principal flux or melter. With clay, the refractory contents, alumina and silica, are preponderant. With glazes, more of the basic oxides like the feldspars are combined with silica to lower the melting temperature of the glaze to fuse it, binding it to the clay body.

Glazes are made up of glass-forming compounds:

Melters or Fluxes	Basic Oxides
Sodium	Na_2O
Potassium	K_2O
Calcium	CaO
Lead	PbO
Zinc	ZnO
Barium	BaO
Magnesium	MgO

Stiffeners	Neutral Oxides
Alumina, which is found in clay	Al_2O_3

Glass-Former	Acid Oxide
Silica or Flint	SiO_2

These oxides are combined in differing amounts to yield glazes that will melt at many different temperatures. The melters lower the firing temperature of the *silica. Usually the sodium and potassium are combined in most of the feldspars. Very often suppliers will include a page in their catalog that gives the chemical analysis for their feldspars.*

You will find as you become more interested in glaze formulation that there are many more other raw glaze materials than those we have touched on here. After you have purchased your glaze materials,

take one tablespoon of each material, add a little water, making a creamy mixture, mix, and paint them on a large bisque slab. Write their names under each slab with iron oxide. Fire the slab at the temperature in which you have decided to work, cone 6, or 8, or 9. The iron will become black and fuse onto the clay. Which ingredient stayed powdery? Which dry? Did any of them flux even a little? What did the coloring oxides do?

Have some test tiles ready for testing some combinations. Start with silica and feldspar.

Tile 1: one part silica, one part feldspar.
Tile 2: one part silica, three parts feldspar.
Tile 3: three parts silica, one part feldspar.
Fire these and observe the results. Is one runny? If so, add a little stiffener, clay. Is one very dry? Try adding a little of another flux and some clay. Keep a clear record of what you add or subtract. You may end up with a very nice glaze.

You may already be endowed with several glaze for-

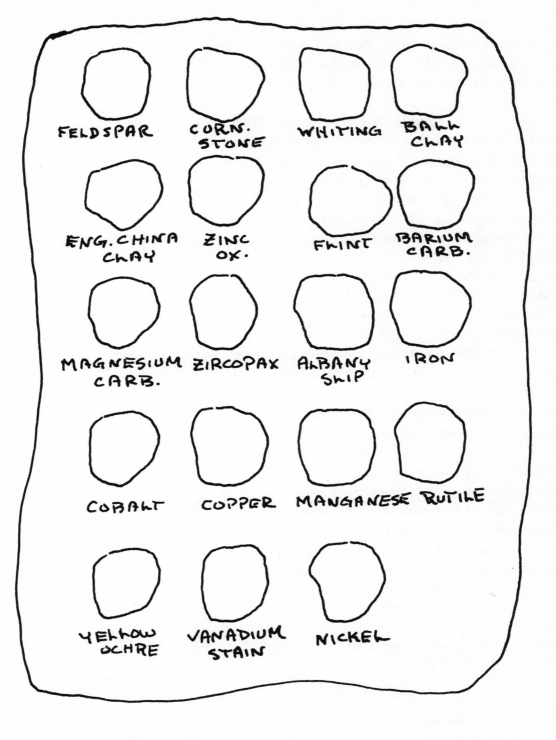

mulas of the temperature range in which you will be firing. But maybe you have not yet had a chance to fire them. An excellent way to test several glazes at once is to

take a bisque cylinder and pour each base glaze (with no colorants) on it vertically, slightly overlapping them around the pot. You can have as many as eight glazes. Then take every one of your coloring oxides and paint a band of each one around the pot covering every glaze. This will show you both the texture of the glaze and how the coloring oxides are affected by each glaze.

You can find some beautiful glazes by doing such a broad-scale test. You will surely become interested in at least one of the glazes on your test cylinder and will want to do color tests for it. You should have two or three dozen little square bisque tiles ready to use for testing. It is also a good idea to prepare several little test bowls. An excellent way to find more colors for a base glaze is to do an equal blend, in which oxides will be mixed into the glaze the way cobalt and copper were mixed into the Albany slip.

First, study this table describing generally the color each percentage of oxide will give in a glaze:

Chrome Oxide	*1 to 2 percent*	*bright green*
Cobalt Oxide	*1 percent*	*bright blue*
	2 percent	*dark blue*
	3 percent	*black*
Copper Oxide	*1 percent*	*light green*
	3 percent	*very dark green*

Iron	2 percent	tan
	4 percent	brown
	6 percent	dark brown
Manganese Carbonate	4 percent	purplish brown
Nickel	2 percent	soft tan, gray. (This oxide is very interesting in glazes.)
Rutile	6 percent	soft tan
Granular Rutile	6 percent	soft speckled tan
Vanadium Stain	8 percent	yellow

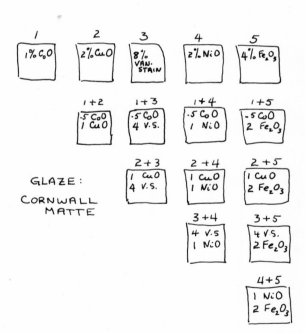

These percentages are not totally accurate because some oxides are affected differently by different glazes.

Choose any five oxides, changing their percentages if you wish for the glaze of your choice. Mix five separate hundred-gram batches of glaze and add a percentage of one oxide to each. Add water and sieve each batch. Take five tiles and number them. In your notebook, keep a record of the name and formula of the glaze, and the oxide percentages. Apply the glazes to each tile. Then take equal amounts, perhaps a tablespoon, of tile 1 glaze plus tile 2 glaze. Mix thoroughly and apply to another tile. This tile will then be an equal amount of 1 and 2, or half a percent cobalt and one percent copper—a new color. Do the same with 1 plus 3, 1 plus 4, and 1 plus 5, etc. This method gives all the possible combinations between 1 and 5, and each tile is a new color.

Once you have all these colors, you may find that you like some of the hues, but you want to see what they would be like a little lighter. The line blend is a way of finding different values of a color.

Weigh out a batch glaze of one hundred grams with the colorants in it, and one batch without colorants. Take five test tiles and dip one in the no-color batch, one in the color batch.

To find the middle color (#3), mix equal amounts of color with no color and apply to the tile. To find #4, mix three parts color to one part no color. For #2, mix one part color to three parts no color.

You can vary this test by putting coloring oxides in both batches, thereby finding relationships in the percentages of oxides.

1	2	3	4	5
NO COLOR	1.25 % CuO .25 CoO 1.25 NiO	1 % CuO .5 CoO 1 NiO	1.5 % CuO .75 CoO 1.5 NiO	2 % CuO 1 % CoO 2 % NiO
	$\frac{1}{4}$ of #5	$\frac{1}{2}$ of #5	$\frac{3}{4}$ of #5	

1	2	3	4	5
4 % Fe_2O_3	3 % Fe_2O_3 .25 CoO	2 % Fe_2O_3 .5 CoO	1 % Fe_2O_3 .75 CoO	1 CoO
	$\frac{1}{4}$ of #5 $\frac{3}{4}$ of #1	$\frac{1}{2}$ of #1 #5	$\frac{1}{4}$ of #1 $\frac{3}{4}$ of #5	

Finally, there is a test you can do rather intuitively.

Mix up as many batches of glaze with colorants as you want, and simply apply them overlapping each other. I usually like to do this test on little bowls so I can more

TEMPERATURE EQUIVALENTS FOR ORTON STANDARD PYROMETRIC CONES

AS DETERMINED AT THE NATIONAL BUREAU OF STANDARDS

| Cone Number | Large Cones | | | | Cone Number | Small Cones | |
	¹60°C	108°F	150°C	270°F		300°C	540°F
015	790	1454	804	1479	015	843	1549
014	834	1533	838	1540	014	870*	1596
013	869	1596	852	1566	013	880*	1615
012	866	1591	884	1623	012	900*	1650
011	886	1627	894	1641	011	915*	1680
†010	887	1629	894	1641	†010	919	1686
09	915	1679	923	1693	09	955	1751
08	945	1733	955	1751	08	983	1801
07	973	1783	984	1803	07	1008	1846
06	991	1816	999	1830	06	1023	1873
05	1031	1888	1046	1915	05	1062	1944
04	1050	1922	1060	1940	04	1098	2008
03	1086	1987	1101	2014	03	1131	2068
02	1101	2014	1120	2048	02	1148	2098
01	1117	2043	1137	2079	01	1178	2152
1	1136	2077	1154	2109	1	1179	2154
2	1142	2088	1162	2124	2	1179	2154
3	1152	2106	1168	2134	3	1196	2185
4	1168	2134	1186	2167	4	1209	2208
5	1177	2151	1196	2185	5	1221	2230
6	1201	2194	1222	2232	6	1255	2291
7	1215	2219	1240	2264	7	1264	2307
8	1236	2257	1263	2305	8	1300	2372
9	1260	2300	1280	2336	9	1317	2403
10	1285	2345	1305	2381	10	1330	2426
11	1294	2361	1315	2399	11	1336	2437
12	1306	2383	1326	2419	12	1355	2471

| Cone Number | | | | | Cone Number | P. C. E. Cones | |
						150°C	270°F
12	1306°C.	2383°F.	1326°C.	2419°F.	12	1337°C.	2439°F.
13	1321	2410	1346	2455	13	1349	2460
14	1388	2530	1366	2491	14	1398	2548
15	1424	2595	1431	2608	15	1430	2606

* Temperatures approximate. See Note 3.
† Iron-free (white) are made in numbers 010 to 3. The iron-free cones have the same deformation temperatures as the red equivalents when fired at a rate of 60 Centigrade degrees per hour in air.

Notes:

1. The temperature equivalents in this table apply only to Orton Standard Pyrometric Cones, *when heated at the rates indicated, in an air atmosphere.*

2. Temperature Equivalents are given in degrees Centigrade (°C.) and the corresponding degrees Fahrenheit (°F.). The rates of heating shown at the head of each column of temperature equivalents were maintained during the last several hundred degrees of temperature rise.

3. The temperature equivalents were determined at the National Bureau of Standards by H. P. Beerman (See Journal of the American Ceramic Society, Vol. 39, 1956), with the exception of those marked (*).

4. The temperature equivalents are not necessarily those at which cones will deform under firing conditions different from those under which the calibrating determinations were made. For more detailed technical data, please write the Orton Foundation.

5. For reproducible results, care should be taken to insure that the cones are set in a plaque with the bending face at the correct angle of 8° from the vertical, with the cone tips at the correct height above the top of the plaque. (Large Cone 2″, small and P.C.E. cones ¹⁵/₁₆″)

6. Permission to reproduce all or any part of this table may be obtained by writing to the Foundation.

clearly see the overlap. Very often two glazes over-lapping will produce a beautiful result.

I strongly recommend that you keep Daniel Rhodes's Clay and Glazes for the Potter *in your studio. It is a very clear presentation of clays, glazes and glaze calculations.*
Glazes can take up a lifetime of work. I don't feel you need to spend your life working on them, but I do think it is worth it to put effort into tests. This is the way you are going to learn about glazes and their effects. The more you experience glazing the more you will want to learn about it.

part

3

Your Studio

Planning

I am not concerned with whether or not you are going to become a professional potter in the sense that you will be earning your living by making pottery. You may say to yourself, "I'm only going to be spending weekends on pottery," or "I have a full-time job and I want to do some pottery on the side," or "I think I may eventually do full-time pottery." At whatever level you decide to work, you need to plan a work space for yourself. This work space is your studio. It can be a room in your house, your garage, a corner of your cellar, a storefront, a factory space, a barn, or any other kind of space you may have available to you. But it is very important that whatever space you have feels good to you—that it is a space you can settle into and in which you can function. Once you can become excited about this space, you can start moving in.

No matter how tiny the room, you must have shelves

for greenware and bisqueware, and some kind of table for handbuilding and glazing. Next to your wheel should be a bench or little table or shelf to hold freshly thrown pots. Wherever the kiln is put (at this point I'm thinking of an electric kiln, which will probably be close to the switch box), there must also be some shelves to hold the ware going into and coming out of the kiln as well as kiln shelves and kiln furniture. If it is at all possible, have a little glaze area, separate from the clay area, for glazing pots, mixing glazes, and doing tests, with a worktable and shelves, and finally, a corner for storing bags of clay and raw glaze materials. A slip bucket for reclaiming dry clay and some kind of wedging board should be placed where they are most convenient to you.

If you are lucky and have a large space in which to work, then a display area is a must. This area, however small, should be simply and handsomely designed, with your work tastefully displayed.

Equipment and Materials

Buying equipment and materials is very often dependent on the money you have available. If the timing is right and you are lucky enough to be there when someone wants to sell out a whole studio, then you can save a few hundred dollars by buying secondhand equipment that is still in good condition. The most essential equipment is, of course, a wheel and a kiln. The necessary initial materials are clay and raw glaze ingredients and/or commercially mixed glazes, which are much more expensive per pound than raw materials. Your tools are a gram and a pound scale, a sixty-to-one-hundred mesh *sieve, some clay tools. These are the minimum essentials.*

Material	Approximate Cost
Wheel (new)	$200 to $450
Electric Kiln (18″ x 18″ x 18″)	$250 to $400
Kiln Shelves	$25 to $50
Stoneware	
Silicon Carbide	
(for temperatures over	
cone 6)	
Kiln Posts	$10 to $20
Pyrometric Cones	$2 to $5
Gram Scale	$15 to $40
Pound Scale	$2 to $5
60- to 100-Mesh Sieve	$10 to $15
Clay	9¢ to 12¢ per pound
Glaze Materials	10¢ to 15¢ per pound
Clay Tools	$2 to $5
Brushes for Glazing	$5

Before buying a wheel and a kiln (both electric and gas fire), it would be wise to research the available commercial companies, who are happy to send you information, to talk to some people who already have equipment, and even to go for advice to the local colleges and schools with pottery departments. When you are looking for a potter's wheel, be sure that you finally decide on a wheel with which you can feel physically comfortable. For example, some people find they are either too tall or too short for most commercial kick wheels. Some people need to stand while they pot, so they would prefer a table model or a wheel that could be put on a high stand. Others like to straddle the wheel—several variable-speed models are designed for this. I wish to caution you against the temptations of wanting to save money and therefore choosing inferior equipment. Even if your venture into pottery-making will be on a part-time basis, I feel that is not reason enough for purchasing mediocre equipment. At the moment that you are doing pottery, I hope that you will be doing it fully and with enough commitment to that moment for you to feel that the time given to it (however limited that may be) is worth a good wheel. To pay a hundred to a hundred and fifty dollars for a wheel that may stop at the slightest pressure is not only a bad investment but it will mean hours of frustration and dissatisfaction with your equipment. If you genuinely cannot afford to think this way, then, of course, you will do what you must to practice your art.

Many people make their own kick wheels from commercial kits or by finding the parts themselves and assembling them. This is the cheapest way to make a wheel.

Electric kilns come with different firing temperature capacities. I feel that regardless of what temperature range you think you will be firing at, it is most practical to have a high-fire kiln. Companies give detailed information about their kilns upon request. It would also be very helpful if you could find people to talk to who are using electric kilns. Here is a list of things you should be aware of once you decide to look for a kiln:

1. The maximum firing temperature (usually this

ranges between 2285 and 2400 degrees Fahrenheit).

2. The size of the kiln on the inside (16" x 16" x 17", 18" x 18" x 18", etc.).

3. The already existing wiring in the place where the kiln will be installed. Is it adequate for the demands of the kiln, and if not, can you bring in the necessary wiring?

4. The outside dimensions of the kiln compared with the dimensions of the doorways through which it must be brought.

5. Does the kiln have legs? If not, prepare some legs of bricks or cement blocks to raise it for air circulation.

6. Is there some ventilation in the room where the kiln will be fired?

7. If the kiln is to be installed against a wall, can you put some kind of insulation (such as asbestos) on the wall if it is wooden?

8. How far away is the kiln from your work space? Is this going to make stacking a difficult matter?

Pyrometric cone: a small cone of clay that will melt and bend at a certain temperature, indicating when the firing is finished.

I feel it is important to install a pyrometer on your kiln. This will help you to learn about its firing speed, and will relate the actual temperature reading in your kiln to the pyrometric cones you are using in the kiln. It takes a few firings to get to know your kiln. I've heard some people say they have been able to fire their kiln to cone 8 in four hours and others say of the same make kiln that they couldn't fire to cone 8 in less than eight hours. Also, keep a diary of every firing—the time of firing, the temperature, the cooling time, the temperature at which you open the kiln, and what you find inside the kiln. The temperature should not be any higher than 300 degrees at the time of opening. If you cool your kiln too abruptly, this will put a strain on the elements and the bricks. Constant fast cooling will shorten the life of your kiln.

It is fine if you wish to invest in an automatic shutoff system, but I must caution you to make it a habit never to leave the kiln to shut off by itself without being aware of the approximate shutoff time and being on the premises at that time. Automatic shutoffs are not foolproof. When you get your kiln, study the instruction booklet carefully, following the firing directions until you become thoroughly familiarized with your kiln.

If you have either the indoor or the outdoor space, you may prefer to have a gas-fired kiln, which you can purchase or build. But there are some things that must be investigated before you establish your kiln.

1. If this is to be an indoor kiln in a town or a city, does the space meet the qualifications of the building and grounds code of that town? If you are building in an isolated place in the country, you may not have to take this into consideration.

2. Is this a space the fire department can approve?

3. Is there natural gas available nearby?

4. Is this a space the town gas inspector can approve?

5. Is there a place in the building through which a

Catenary arch kiln
built by Tom Joanides.

chimney can be built from the kiln leading outside? If so, have the fire department approve it.
If the kiln is to be built outdoors, and there are
buildings and trees near the area, then the above
considerations must also be taken into account.
The placement of the chimney is a matter that
should be discussed with the fire department.

*If you are going to use liquid propane, then the local
gas company will have to install the connecting pipes
from the gas tanks to the burners. From then on, you
have established a lasting relationship with your gas-
man. Whenever you fire the kiln, it would be helpful to
keep an accurate record of how much each firing costs,
although your bills will also tell you that.*

Firing

*Before doing your first glaze-firing, you must prepare
the kiln and the shelves by painting a coating of kiln
wash on the floor of the kiln and on the top of the
shelves. Kiln wash can be bought already prepared or
you can make your own by mixing an equal amount
each of clay and flint and adding just enough water for
a thick, fluid mix. Kiln wash makes it easier to chip off
any glaze that may accidentally flow off a pot. Your kiln
furniture and kiln floor must always be kept clean and
freshly painted.*
*An excellent way to get a good feeling of how to
stack a kiln is to draw the shelf dimensions on a table
and arrange pots in this space as tightly as you can,
allowing room for posts. If it is a bisque-firing you are*

Right: Sprung arch kiln
built by author and Kathleen Ingoldsby.

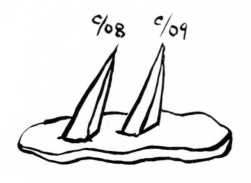

planning, pots can touch each other and be stacked on top of one another. When stacking pots within one another, care must be taken that the inside pot is not much heavier than the outside one, or that the two pots upon shrinking in the firing do not lock together.

A good temperature for bisquing is between cone 010 and 07. If you don't have an automatic shutoff, always have cone pads ready for your firing. For a bisque, put a cone 09 in front of an 08. The 09 will melt first. For a glaze, cone 7 in front of cone 8, or 8 in front of 9. The lower numbers will melt first. The cone pads should be

161

placed inside the kiln near the peepholes, so you can observe the cones bending at the height of the firing. It is a good idea when firing to leave the kiln on low with the cover open for at least two hours. This will dry the pots slowly and allow moisture to escape more freely. Then close the cover for one hour before putting the switches to the next level. I feel in a bisque-firing that the drying time should always take several hours. I've even left my kiln on low with the cover open overnight. Then, when the cone bends, allow plenty of time for cooling—ten to twelve hours—until you can put your hand into the kiln and touch the pots without burning yourself. By allowing time for cooling, you avoid straining the elements and bricks by erratic temperature changes and the life of the kiln is prolonged. When it does come time to install new elements or new switches, however, most kiln manufacturers will supply you with clear instructions on how to do this.

Stacking a glaze kiln is more critical than stacking a bisque. Pots with a glaze on them must not touch one another or they will fuse together. Therefore, fewer pots will fit into a glaze kiln. Tips on stacking a glaze:

1. Pots should be an eighth to a fourth of an inch from each other.

2. All pots should stand flat on the kiln floor or shelf. Do not put stilts under a pot if you fire stoneware temperatures. At these temperatures the pot will slump down over the stilts.

3. Do not have a wide-bottomed pot hang over the edge. It will slump.

4. Always have the first shelf at least four inches

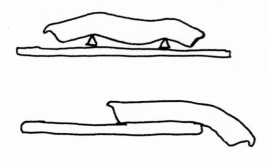

from the kiln floor to allow for heat circulation.

5. In the first few firings, place cone pads in several parts of the kiln to determine evenness of firing.

6. Always keep an accurate account or graph of every firing, even the bisque, indicating time and temperature. If you do not have a pyrometer, keep an account of the number of hours for each temperature setting, that is, how many hours on low, medium, high. These records can be helpful when it comes time to repair your kiln.

7. Be sure to cool the kiln slowly. If a pot is strained by abrupt temperature changes, it will shatter, sometimes long after it is removed from the kiln. You will notice, if pots are taken out of the kiln while they are still very hot, they will ping as they adjust to the cooler room temperature.

The same things hold true for stacking a gas kiln, which is very often a front loader. The firing, of course, depends on the design of the kiln, and is not as automatic as the firing of an electric kiln.*

Studio Rhythm

The manner in which you work in your studio and the time you spend there depends on the kind of commitment you have given to pottery and the time and space you have been able to allow in your life for the doing of pottery. Obviously, if you have purchased equipment and materials, you are committed. The rhythm of working is up to you. I strongly advise, however, that you

*Refer to: Kilns, Daniel Rhodes

10/14/72

COVERED POT

VICTOR WHITE INSIDE.
BIRD MATTE OUT.

4 PLANTERS

BIRD MATTE OUT.

PLANTER

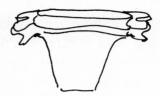

HAMADA TOP.
NO GLAZE BOTTOM.

GOBLET

VICTOR WHITE IN.
ALUMINA OUT.
IRON DESIGN OVER.

LARGE BOWL

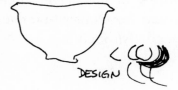

DESIGN

VICTOR WHITE IN & OUT.
COBALT DESIGN IN.
WAX OVER DESIGN.
IRON DESIGN OVER ALL.
IRON SPRAY WHOLE POT.

work in a consistent way, setting for yourself tasks and goals. It is fun as well as informative to keep a journal of your workday, how many pots you completed, what you learned from a series of pots, how many you destroyed, some designs you worked out, how you feel about them, how you feel about your progress. The journal could be your notebook, in which you keep drawings of ideas, glazes, glaze tests and their results. I like to record every glaze load by drawing the pot, describing it, and describing the glazes and glaze technique. For example see opposite.

Test pots can be recorded in this way also.

How you keep the studio in order and the clay recycled is a matter of how much time you spend there. As you develop your work habits you will also develop studio upkeep. When I leave my studio, I always clean up after myself, even though I am going to be there again the next day. Never let the slip bucket remain full. Clay should be recycled, every day if necessary.

Some studio chores:

1. Recycle the clay.
2. Resieve the glazes before using them.
3. Wash the tools after using them.
4. Sweep the floor around your wheel after tooling.
5. Keep cone pads available for firing.
6. Clean the whole studio once a month.
7. Keep the glaze buckets filled.
8. Keep the kiln floor clean and the shelves freshly painted with kiln wash.

Work freely,
Work energetically, and
Work well.

Suppliers

There are several ways to find out about suppliers near you:

Yellow Pages

1. *Pottery equipment and supplies*
2. *Refractories (for fire brick)*
3. *Clay*
4. *Kilns*
5. *Burners*

Art Schools and Universities with Pottery Departments

Clay, chemicals, kilns, wheels, tools.

Potters

Wheels, kilns, and especially clay and chemicals.

Ceramics Monthly *Magazine*

Or write to Ceramics Monthly, 900 East State Street, Athens, Ohio 45701. Especially for kilns and wheels.

American Crafts Council

Write for information: 44 West 53rd Street, New York, New York 10019.

Schools

For schools, courses, and workshops, inquire:

> *Education Department*
> *American Crafts Council*
> *44 West 53rd Street*
> *New York, New York 10019*

Suggested Books and Publications

Bibliography

Ball, F. Carlton. *Decorating Pottery with Clay, Slip and Glaze.* Columbus, Ohio: Professional Publications, 1967.
Behrens, Richard. *Glaze Projects: A Formulary of Leadless Glazes.* Columbus, Ohio: Professional Publications, 1971.
Berensohn, Paulus. *Finding One's Way with Clay.* New York: Simon & Schuster, 1972.
Clark, Kenneth. *Pottery Throwing for Beginners.* New York: Studio Vista; London: Watson-Guptill Publications, 1970.
Leach, Bernard. *A Potter's Book.* London: Transatlantic Art; New York: Faber & Faber, 1946.
Nelson, Glenn C. *Ceramics: A Potter's Handbook.* New York: Holt, Rinehart & Winston, 1971.
Norton, F. H. *Ceramics for the Artist Potter.* Reading, Massachusetts: Addison-Wesley, 1956.
Rhodes, Daniel. *Clay and Glazes for the Potter.* Toronto: Chilton; Philadelphia: Ambassador Book, 1957.
———. *Kilns: Design, Construction, and Operation.* Philadelphia: Chilton Book, 1968.
Sanders, Herbert H. *The World of Japanese Ceramics.* Palo Alto, California: Kodansha International, 1967.

Publications

Ceramics Monthly: Professional Publications, Inc., Box 4548, Columbus, Ohio 43212. Published monthly except July and August.
Craft Horizons: American Crafts Council, 44 West 53rd Street, New York, New York 10019. Published bimonthly.
Studio Potter: Daniel Clark Foundation, Box 172, Warner, New Hampshire 03278, published biannually.